LIVING WORD! LIVING WATER!

Explorers

YEAR C

Susan Sayers
with Father Andrew Moore

TWENTY-THIRD PUBLICATIONS
BAYARD Mystic, CT 06355

YEAR C

Explorers

First published in 2000 in Great Britain by
KEVIN MAYHEW LTD
Buxhall
Stowmarket
Suffolk IP14 3BW

North American copyright © Susan Sayers 2000
Twenty-Third Publications/ Bayard
185 Willow Street
P.O. Box 180
Mystic, CT 06355
(860) 536-2611
(800) 321-0411

ISBN: 1-58595-104-8
Printed in the U.S.A.

The other titles in the *Living Word! Living Water! Year C* series are

Complete Resource Book   ISBN 1-58595-102-1

Seekers   ISBN 1-58595-103-X

Adventurers   ISBN 1-58595-105-6

Edited by Katherine Laidler
Illustrations by Arthur Baker

Foreword

For children of primary school age the sense of belonging to a peer group becomes increasingly important. Their faith development can be fostered in group activities which are fun and challenging. Their growing awareness of the wider world is often linked with a strong sense of justice and social responsibility, and they need to see the Christian perspective in all this.

Explorers encourages the children to begin thinking about the implications of their faith. Their participation in the story-telling and teaching is welcomed.

It would be wise to split the group into two age groups, adapting the suggestions on the worksheets accordingly.

This is something of a do-it-yourself kit, supplied with plenty of openings to meet your own parish needs and the needs of the children, and to spark off your own imaginative ideas. It is based on the belief that children are as much a part of the Church as adults, and that there is great value in sharing the same teaching each Sunday, whatever our age. This book follows the weekly readings of the Lectionary for Year C of the three-year cycle, so that the whole church will have that common experience.

Explorers includes a series of weekly activity sheets. These may be copied without further permission or charge for non-commercial use. They can be used as they stand, or you can select the material you want. Copy them for the children to take home, use them in church, put them in the magazine or news sheet, or use them in conjunction with any catechetical program. They are "activity sheets" rather than "worksheets" as they often include instructions for making and doing rather than being complete in themselves. Children will need their leaders to have planned ahead for the resources needed.

When planning for children's work it is advisable to read through the Scripture passages prayerfully. You are then in a better position to see how the program relates to the readings, and also to supplement and vary the program as a result of your own insights and the specific needs of your group.

The children are encouraged to pray during the week, using the suggestions on their sheet. These can be built into a collection of prayers and made into a personal prayer book.

A few general ideas about story-telling:

- Tell the story from the viewpoint of a character in the situation. To create the time-machine effect, avoid eye contact as you slowly put on the appropriate cloth or cloak, and then make eye contact as you greet the children in character.

- Have an object with you which leads into the story—a water jug or a lunch box, for instance.

- Walk the whole group through the story, so that they are physically moving from one place to another; and use all kinds of places, such as broom closets, under the stairs, outside under the trees, and so on.

- Collect some carpet squares—blue and green—so that at story time the children can sit around the edge of this and help you place on the cut-outs for the story.

You may find it useful to keep a record of what you actually do each week, as well as build up a store of the resources you use, because this will obviously help to make future activities easier to prepare.

It is our hope that this book will not only stimulate ideas and enable a varied program of children's work to take place, but most of all it will encourage us all, whatever our age, as we make the journey of faith together.

SUSAN SAYERS
with Father Andrew Moore

Contents

Teaching programs and activity sheets for the following Special Feasts will be found in the *Explorers* book for Year A.

Mary, Mother of God—January 1

The Presentation of the Lord (Candlemas)—February 2

Saint John the Baptist—June 24

Saints Peter and Paul—June 29

The Transfiguration of the Lord—August 6

The Assumption—August 15

The Triumph of the Holy Cross—September 14

All Saints—November 1

Feasts of the Dedication of a Church

This book is dedicated to my family and friends,
whose encouraging support has been wonderful,
and to all those whose good ideas are included here for others to share.

Advent

First Sunday
of Advent

Thought for the day

The gathered hopes of generations remind us to get ourselves ready, so that Christ's return will be a day of excitement and great joy.

Readings

Jeremiah 33:14–16
1 Thessalonians 3:12—4:2
Luke 21:25–28, 34–36

Aim: To help them understand that at Christmas we also look ahead to the second coming.

Starter

Split the group in two (or four if numbers are larger) and give the members of each group short strands of yarn or string in their group's color. All the children now drop or hide their yarn or string all around the room. Now ask each group to find and collect a different color. (First group back wins, if you want to add some competition.)

Teaching

Remind the children of how, when they were gathering up the yarn or string they were looking out for a particular type of yarn or string, and only collecting that. We'll come back to this later.

They will all be aware that Christmas is approaching, and that we celebrate Jesus coming to live on earth as a human baby at that time. Enjoy the thought of Christmas coming.

Explain that while he was on earth, Jesus told us he would come back again one day and we will all be able to see him then. Make it quite clear that we have not been told when this will happen, and read Luke 21:25–28; 34–36, asking them to listen for the signs to notice. Readers will find it helpful to follow the words using the activity sheet.

Have a short "Any questions?" break at this point.

Now go back to the yarn/string gathering. At this second coming, all that is or has been good, honest, generous, kind, forgiving and loving will be gathered up, and will last forever. Jesus suggests that we make sure we are ready for this, so we can enjoy being part of the harvest.

Praying

Using the sprinter's action for "On your mark…get set…go!" have the children line up and crouch down, then follow these cues:

Take me as I am, Lord Jesus,
> (*raise themselves to the "get set" position*)
make me more loving/forgiving/honest,
> (*and run to the opposite wall*)
and use me for good!

Activities

Use the activity sheet to work on ways to get ready and prepare for the time when all things will be fulfilled.

Notes

Jesus will come again in glory

I want to be ready. I need God to help me with

To pray at home this week

Take me as I am,
Lord Jesus, make
me more loving
and use me
for good.   Amen.

Do you think this is good news or bad news?

Underline the signs to notice in red.
Underline what people will see in blue.
Jesus says 'don't fear'.
Why don't we need to be afraid?
Underline the reason in green.

Jesus said this:

'Amazing things will happen to the sun, moon and stars. On earth the nations will be afraid because of the roar and fury of the sea. They will not know what to do. People will be so afraid they will faint. They will wonder what is happening to the whole world. Everything in the sky will be changed.

Then people will see the Son of Man coming in a cloud with power and great glory.

When these things begin to happen don't fear. Look up and hold your heads high because the time when your God will free you is near!'

Second Sunday
of Advent

Thought for the day

It had been prophesied that there would be a messenger to prepare the way for the coming of the Messiah. Now John the Baptist appears with his urgent message of repentance.

Readings

Baruch 5:1–9
Philippians 1:4–6, 8–11
Luke 3:1–6

Aim: To understand that John was the prophesied forerunner to prepare the people for the Messiah.

Starter

Advance notice. Have a selection of posters and flyers for local events (you might find some of these in your local newspaper). Have some with pictures to help non-readers. Hang the posters at different places on the walls and give the children a minute to walk around and look at them. Then have everyone move into the center of the room. Call out: "Did you know there was going to be a circus (or carnival, or grand opening, or whatever is happening in your area) next Saturday?" The children run to the appropriate poster.

Teaching

Beforehand prepare a poster that says: "Good news—don't miss it! The Messiah is coming!" and a sign with a string attached saying "John the Baptist."

Explain that for thousands of years people had known that one day God would come among his people on earth in a very close way. The people of Israel were waiting for the day when the Messiah would appear on earth. (Display the poster.) Everyone can shout out together: "The name 'Messiah' means 'the chosen one' or 'the Christ'." But God didn't rely on posters: he had a better idea. He chose a personal messenger.

At this point one of the leaders interrupts to say that she wants to give advance notice of a children's Christmas party/carol singing (or whatever exciting event you have planned for Christmas). The excitement generated by this will enable you to show how effective it is to have a personal messenger. Explain that the name of the personal messenger God chose was John, known as John the Baptist. (Hang the sign around the messenger's neck.)

What was John's message?

God told John to tell the people that to get ready for the coming Messiah, they needed to put their crooked lives straight. Their lives needed to be like clear firm roads. That meant sorting out all lying and cheating, all cruel and unkind behavior, all mean and selfish living. The people wanted to get ready for the Messiah, so they wanted to sort their lives out. This turning away from sin is called "repentance." As a sign that their sins had been forgiven, John baptized the people in the water of the River Jordan. The people felt happy and free. It feels good to be forgiven.

Praying

Have everyone stand and face in the same direction. Whenever the leader says *"Turn us around,"* the children turn around and continue with the prayer.

Father, whenever we are wanting our own way,
    Turn us around to think of other people.

Whenever we know we are not being honest,
    Turn us around to speak the truth.

Whenever we find ourselves being greedy,
    Turn us around to share with others.

Thanks for helping, Lord.
Amen.

Activities

Use the activity sheet to reinforce today's teaching and express the message of John in poster form for the rest of the congregation.

> ### Notes

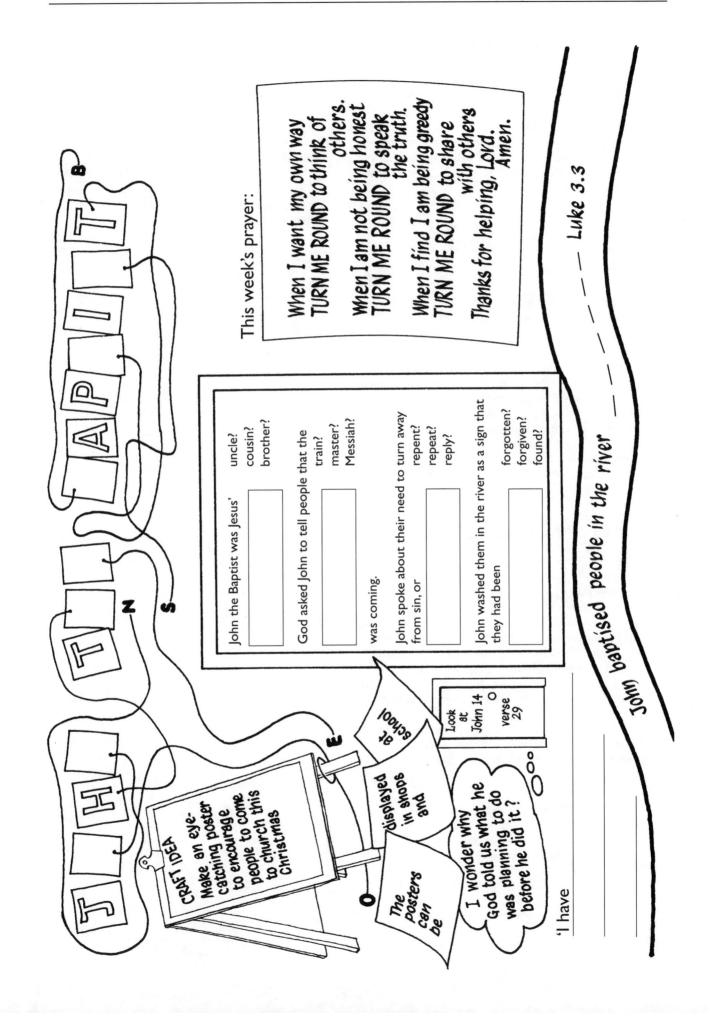

JOHN THE BAPTIST

This week's prayer:

When I want my own way
TURN ME ROUND to think of others.
When I am not being honest
TURN ME ROUND to speak the truth.
When I find I am being greedy
TURN ME ROUND to share with others
Thanks for helping, Lord. Amen.

John the Baptist was Jesus'
uncle?
cousin?
brother?

God asked John to tell people that the
train?
master?
Messiah?
was coming.

John spoke about their need to turn away from sin, or
repent?
repeat?
reply?

John washed them in the river as a sign that they had been
forgotten?
forgiven?
found?

CRAFT IDEA
Make an eye-catching poster to encourage people to come to church this Christmas

The posters can be displayed in shops and at school

I wonder why God told us what he was planning to do before he did it?

Look at John 14 verse 29

'I have

John baptised people in the river

— — — Luke 3.3

Third Sunday of Advent

Thought for the day

Our period of preparation shifts from repentance and forgiveness to the freed exhilaration of hope, as the momentous truth of God's immanence begins to dawn on us.

Readings

Zephaniah 3:14–18
Philippians 4:4–7
Luke 3:10–18

Aim: To develop their understanding from last week about the importance of John as the forerunner to Christ.

Starter

Name and throw. Stand in a circle with a beach ball. Call out the name of someone else in the circle and then throw the ball to them. Remind them beforehand to see if they can make sure that everyone has at least one go. This activity helps build community, includes new children, and picks up on the fact that being chosen and called gets you ready to receive.

Teaching

Get the children to help recap the teaching from last week about who John was and why he was called the Baptist.

Have two leaders discussing what had gone on by the River Jordan when they were there in the crowd. One is a soldier and one a tax collector. To be able to do this effectively they will need to be very familiar with the Luke text and practice beforehand so that the conversation sounds natural and interesting, while bringing out a) the teaching that John has given and b) their excitement about waiting for this other person John has told them to look out for.

Following the conversation, draw out the main points from the children, noting them on a flipchart, board or overhead projector.

Praying

Copy this prayer and hand it out so everyone can join in:

Leader   What do we want?

All   We want to be ready!

Leader   When do we want it?

All   Now!

Leader   Who can help us?

All   God can help us!

Leader   When can he help us?

All   Now!

Activities

Today's activity sheet helps the children test their understanding of the events at the River Jordan by placing them in their historical context. They can also make a stand-up model.

Notes

1 Find the River Jordan in an atlas.

2 What country is it in now?

3 Who was in charge when John was alive?

What did John say to the soldiers?

What did John say to the tax collectors?

How to make the pop-up picture
1 Color the picture
2 Cut out the people in the water, leaving the fold lines
3 Fold the back and people up like this

B	R	I	S	P	N	F	B
E	E	G	F	R	E	E	A
G	P	L	I	T	N	H	P
N	E	C	I	A	R	M	T
A	N	K	D	V	J	Q	I
H	T	R	I	V	E	R	S
C	O	O	L	D	S	E	T
J	O	H	N	U	A	P	E

JOHN the BAPTIST called people to REPENT and CHANGE what was wrong in their lives, so they could be SET FREE to LIVE. To show they were forgiven John baptized them in the RIVER JORDAN.

This week's prayer

Please Jesus help me to do whatever is right and good and honest today. *Amen.*

Time Line

2000
Abraham lived

0
Jesus lived

Romans took charge

2000
you live

Fourth Sunday of Advent

Thought for the day
Amazing things happen when we cooperate with God.

Readings
Micah 5:1–4
Hebrews 10:5–10
Luke 1:39–45

Aim: To explore what it meant for Mary to say "Yes."

Starter
Either join with the younger children for parachute games, or have a team game which needs team members to cooperate (e.g., soccer, or a relay race, or pass the balloon between the knees).

Teaching
Find out if anyone has ever played on a sports team or in an orchestra, or sung in the choir. Have some pictures of well-known athletes and actors as well. Talk about how pleased and proud you feel to be asked to do an important job, but bring out the point that you can't just go along to play in the match or act in the performance. What other things would you have to do? List both the up and the down sides of such a privilege. Looking at it as a whole, would they still want to take it on? (You could all vote on it.)

Have another sheet with a picture of Mary in the middle. At the top of the sheet write "Chosen to be Jesus' mother."

Look at what Mary was chosen for, and on one side of the picture list all the good things about her life. Then think about Jesus' life and see if you can think of any sad, painful, or difficult things that were part of it. List these on the other side of the picture. Now ask how the children would feel about taking on the job of being God's mother.

At the bottom write, "Mary still said 'Yes!'" It amazed her that God had chosen her, and it made her realize how wonderful and sensible and patient and courageous God was to set about saving the world in this way.

Mary went to visit her cousin Elizabeth, who was six months pregnant with John the Baptist at the time, and both Mary and Elizabeth (and John) were filled with excitement and delight at what God was up to.

Praying
Have some happy music on to dance to and while the music is still playing everyone claps a rhythm and shouts these words to it:

My soul glorifies the Lord
and my spirit rejoices in God my savior.

Activities
Consolidate the teaching using the activity sheet, and follow the instructions on it to make a Christmas table decoration.

Notes

God with us

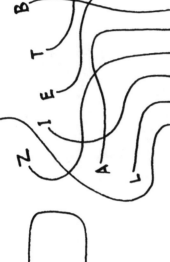

Mary knew it would not be an easy job being the mother of God's son.

But... she still said:

This week's prayer

My soul glorifies the Lord and my Spirit rejoices in God my saviour. Amen

E Z E I T B

□ □ □ □ □ □ □ — H

Mary met _____, her cousin.

They were very happy about what God was doing.

Draw them here

Circle the + Square the −

This will be exciting

Amazing! God is using ME!

The people might reject my son

If God has asked me I know he will help me to do it

This is a mammoth job and I might do it wrong

People will not understand my son

God is keeping his promise to save us

I don't suppose my life will ever be 'normal' now

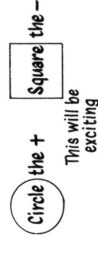

GOD WITH US

A Christmas table decoration

You will need:
• a foil dish   • a candle
• a chunk of oasis
• some holly and ivy
• some garden wire
• shiny colored paper
• putty from a florist

How you make it

1 Cut out circles of shiny paper. Stick them back to back on short pieces of garden wire like this.

2 Fix the oasis in the foil dish with putty.

3 Push the candle and holly and ivy and garden wire berries into the oasis.

4 Decorate the 'God with us' label and stick it on the foil dish.

Christmas

Christmas Day

Thought for the day

Emmanuel—"God with us"—is born at Bethlehem into the human family. Now we will be able to understand, in human terms, what God is really like.

Readings

Note: These readings are for Midnight Mass. Reflections on the readings for the Day Mass are to be found in *Living Word! Living Water! Year A*, and for the Mass at Dawn in *Living Word! Living Water! Year B*.

Isaiah 9:1–6
Titus 2:11–14
Luke 2:1–14

Activities

Christmas Day is very much a time for all God's children to worship together.

Involve all the children in the singing and playing of carols, decorating the church, and in the other ministries of welcoming, serving, collection of gifts and so on.

A coloring activity for today is provided.

Notes

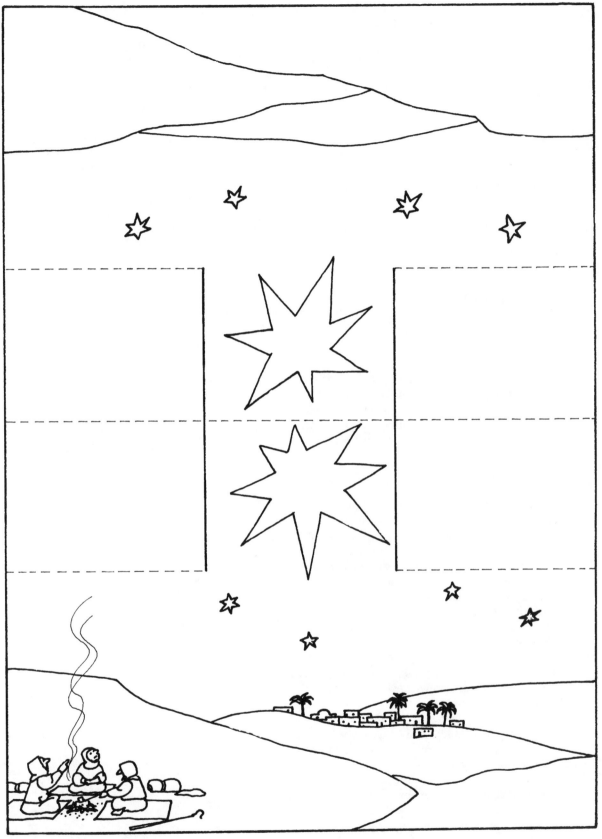

Color, cut out and fold.
Stand on the table for Christmas dinner.

First Sunday of Christmas: The Holy Family

Thought for the day

Jesus' perception and understanding of his purpose and work begins to take shape throughout his childhood in the Holy Family.

Readings

Sirach 3:2–6, 12–14
Colossians 3:12–21
Luke 2:41–52

Aim: To understand that Jesus shared a human childhood, and to look at the kind of experiences he would probably have had.

Starter

Sit in a circle and pass around a toy as each person has a turn to speak. Only the one holding the toy can speak. The first round is "What I liked best about this Christmas was …" Anyone not wanting to speak just passes the toy on. The next round is "The job I hate having to do is …"

Teaching

Have a timeline displayed to help the children place Jesus' birth in its historical context. (Copy this from the timeline drawn on the activity sheet.) Have available some library books, travel brochures and Bibles with pictures of Palestine under the Romans and some photographs of the country surrounding Bethlehem. Have a large flat stone or board to demonstrate grinding flour and kneading dough, and a display of some of the raisins and dates and nuts that would have been grown and eaten.

Give the children a "living museum" experience of what life would have been like for Jesus and his friends, bringing in whatever examples and artifacts you can get hold of. You may for instance be able to borrow some fabric or traditional clothing from the area, or traditional lamps or bedrolls, or you could use the pictures. The more involved the children are the better.

They can find out about sitting crosslegged on the floor and chanting from memory in school, and the kind of local jobs that would be the equivalent of a paper route, such as babysitting, or helping with yardwork.

Praying

Jesus, you know what it's like
to be the same age as me.
Remind me that I can
talk things over with you
whenever I want
and you always
have time to listen. Amen.

Activities

Use the activity sheet to consolidate the teaching, looking at the different areas of life for children in Jesus' time and comparing and contrasting with their own lives. There are suggestions for making a display to put up in church.

Notes

Timeline:

2000	1500	1000	500	0	500	1000	1500	2000
Abraham lived	built in Egypt	King David lived	Greeks ruled	Romans ruled	Jesus lived	Romans left Britain	Greeks ruled	Viking raids on Britain	Columbus sailed to America	You live

Jesus grows up

Jesus and I both ...

- go to school
- drink water
- learn things by heart
- play with our friends
- ride bikes
- eat bread
- get thirsty
- pick fruit
- walk to school
- visit the family
- help at home
- get hungry
- make our bed
- watch the sun set
- do chores
- look after animals

Circle the things you both do.

Make a display. Color enlarged letters from a spare sheet for the title. You will need pictures drawn of

- a house in Nazareth
- a village well
- a palm tree
- bread making
- a map showing Nazareth
- children in school
- a water jug
- a child with sheep

Write about each picture. Stick everything on a large sheet of paper.

This week's prayer

Jesus, you know what it's like to be the same age as me. Remind me that I can talk things over with you whenever I want and you always have time to listen. Amen.

Draw Jesus at school or helping Mom or Dad at home or playing.

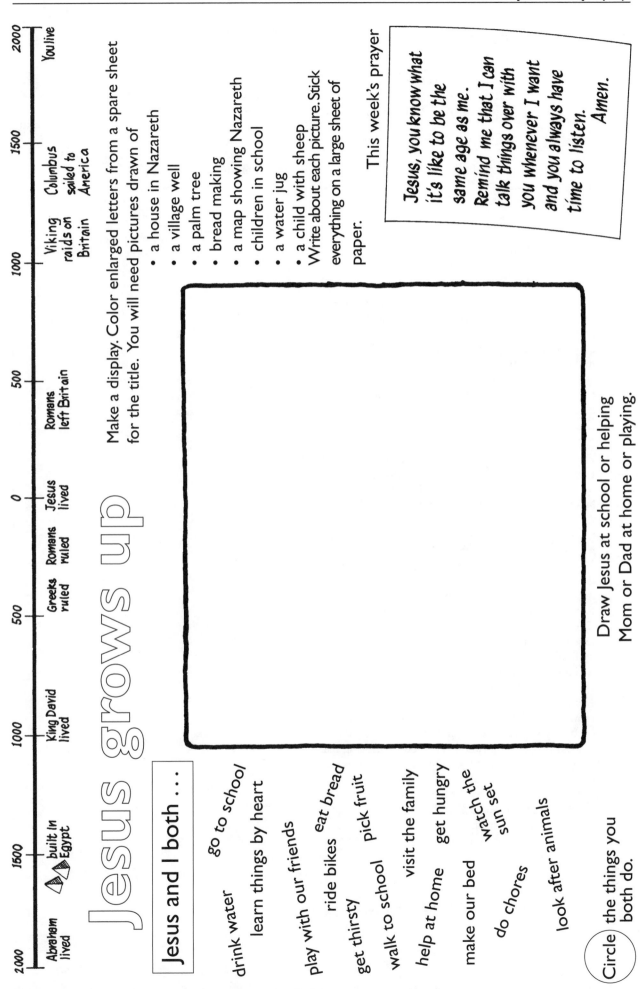

Second Sunday of Christmas

Thought for the day
Christ is the way God tells people about himself.

Readings
Sirach 24:1–2, 8–12
Ephesians 1:3–6, 15–18
John 1:1–18

Aim: To see Jesus as the Word of God.

Starter
Sit in a circle. Name the children in order around the circle: apple, orange, banana. Remove one chair and stand in the middle. Call "banana!" and all the bananas get up and change places, while the person in the center is trying to get a vacated seat. Whoever is left in the middle calls the next fruit, and so on. If the person in the middle calls "fruit salad!" then everyone changes places.

Teaching
Draw attention to the way that in the game the person in the middle made certain things happen by the word they spoke. What other words in our language set things happening? (Words like "Silence!" and "Help!" and "Quick march!") What word was spoken by God to start our world being made? ("Let there be light." They can look it up in Genesis 1 and on the activity sheet.) Read the first three verses of John 1 so that they can see how important God's word, or message, or communication was. If you have these displayed, the older children and better readers will be able to read it together. Or the children can repeat it after you, line by line.

Now read part of today's gospel, starting at verse 14, asking the children to listen out for the word "Word," and try and guess who it means. How can God's Word be in the world?

If they have no idea, remind them that the Word spoken by God at creation was God expressing his love. What person can they think of who expresses God's love, or tells us about God's love? If possible, draw the children to see for themselves that Jesus is the Word of God, rather than telling them outright. All words have power, and God's Word of love is not just sounds, but a person. Jesus is God saying "I love you!"

Praying
Jesus, you are the loving Word of God.
Speak in my life

and help me to listen. Amen.

Activities
The power of words is looked at on the activity sheet, and this leads on to reinforce John's teaching of Jesus expressing God's love in human terms we can understand. Instructions are given for creating a banner on this truth which can be carried into church and displayed for the benefit of the rest of the community.

Notes

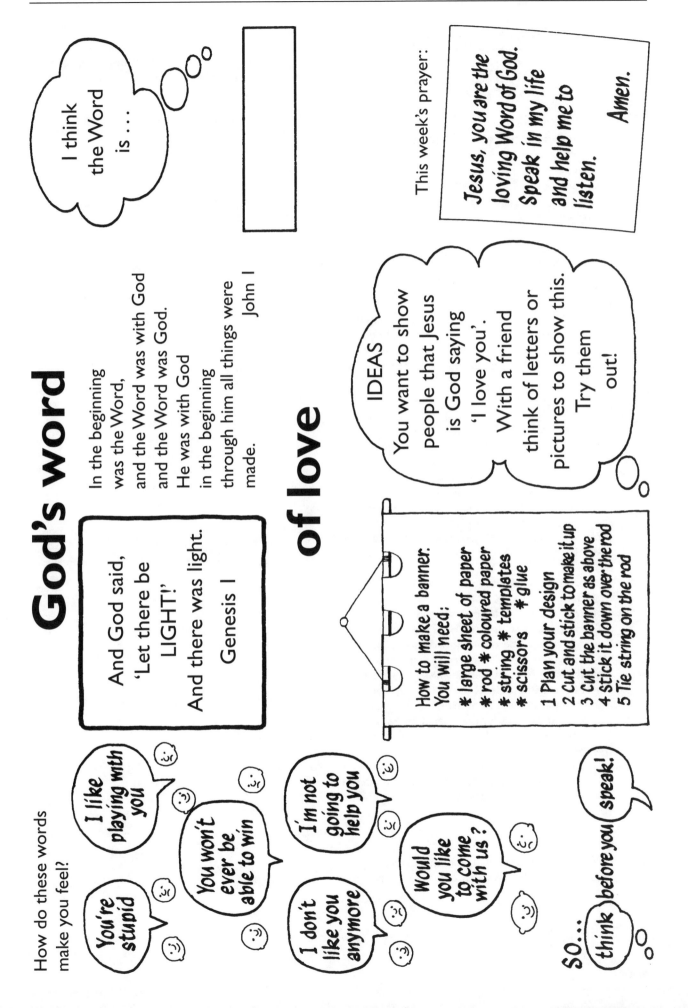

The Epiphany of the Lord

Thought for the day
Jesus, the hope of the nations, is shown to the world.

Readings
Isaiah 60:1–6
Ephesians 3:2–3a, 5–6
Matthew 2:1–12

Aim: To explore why the wise men made their journey and what they found out.

Starter
Who am I? Tape or stick a picture of an animal or food item to everyone's back. They have to find out who they are by going around asking questions about themselves. The others can only answer yes or no.

Teaching
Point out how in the game they had to search for the right answer, and it was like a journey to find the truth. Sometimes people were helpful in that and sometimes they weren't. Today we are looking at some wise men who set out on a quest.

Have two or three adults meeting up as if they are resting on the journey and chatting together about what the day has been like, what they miss, and what they are hoping to find. It is best to try out the conversation beforehand but without any set words as it will then sound natural.

When the wise men have settled down for the night (or gone to feed the camels), show the children a sheet of paper with these headings on it: Who? What? Why? In the different sections brainstorm ideas about who they were (wise men from the East), what they were doing (following a star to find a baby king of great importance) and why they bothered (they had worked out from the signs that this birth was really important for the human race, and they felt a strong urge to be there and pay their respects). Use the children's words, of course.

Now have the wise men on their way back, talking about how they felt about King Herod, what it was like to see Jesus, and why they are going home by a different route.

Praying
Have some incense, gold and myrrh on display during the teaching. As each is brought to the front pray together:

Gold
The wise men brought gold to Jesus.
Jesus, we bring you the gold of our obedience.
Help us to live as you want us to. Amen.

Frankincense
The wise men brought frankincense to Jesus.
Jesus, we bring you the incense of our worship.
You are God and we worship you. Amen.

Myrrh
The wise men brought myrrh to Jesus.
Jesus, we bring you the myrrh of the world's sadness.
Help us to look after one another better. Amen.

Activities
You will need lots of shelf paper or rolls of wallpaper. The best present we can give to Jesus is ourselves. Working in twos, the children draw around each other on the paper, cut themselves out and color them. On the front write:

Jesus,
the best present
I can give you
is myself!

The cut-outs can be offered with the gifts in church and given back at the end of the service for the children to remember at home.

The activity sheet has a sequencing activity to consolidate the teaching, and a look at our own journey to Jesus.

Notes

Color these pictures, cut them out and stick them in the right order . . .

over here

The wise men come to see Jesus

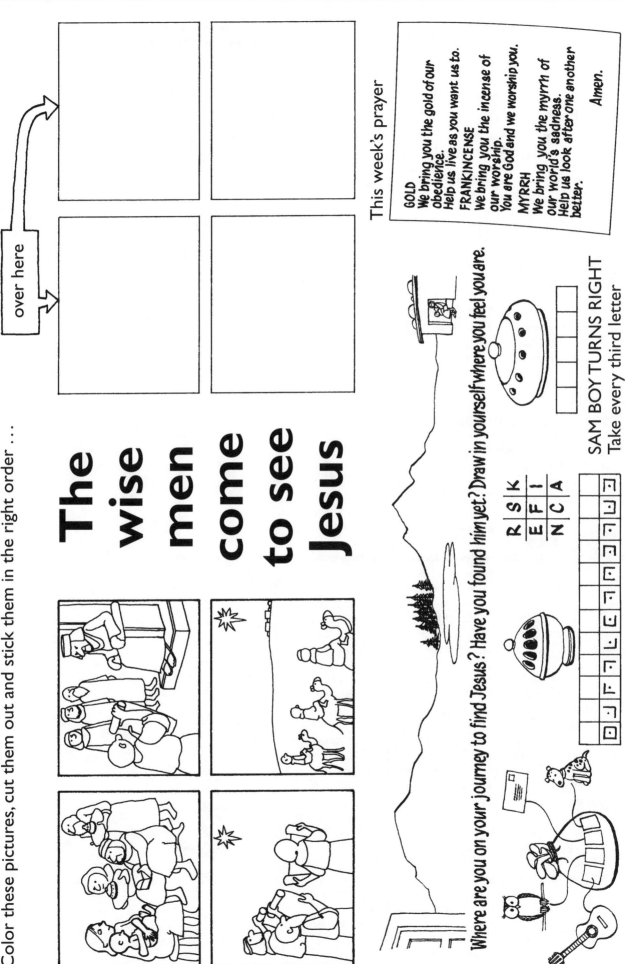

This week's prayer

GOLD
We bring you the gold of our obedience.
Help us live as you want us to.
FRANKINCENSE
We bring you the incense of our worship.
You are God and we worship you.
MYRRH
We bring you the myrrh of our world's sadness.
Help us look after one another better.

Amen.

Where are you on your journey to find Jesus? Have you found him yet? Draw in yourself where you feel you are.

R	S	K
E	F	t
N	C	A

SAM BOY TURNS RIGHT
Take every third letter

The Baptism of the Lord

Thought for the day

Jesus is baptized, and God confirms his identity and his calling.

Readings

Isaiah 42:1–4, 6–7
Acts 10:34–38
Luke 3:15–16, 21–22

Aim: To get to know the story of Jesus' Baptism according to Luke.

Starter

Show pictures of famous people and characters from books, and see how many everyone can identify. Or they can match names with pictures.

Teaching

Bring along some Baptism certificates (a mixture of old and recent ones) and any other signs of Baptism that your church or the children's families have, such as robes, special candles, cards and presents to mark the occasion. It is a very special and important day for us because when we are baptized with water in the name of God the Father, Son and Holy Spirit, we are called by name to follow Jesus, and we decide to follow the Christian way of life.

Today we are going to look at what happened when Jesus was baptized in the River Jordan. Spread out the carpet squares, or ground- and sky-colored sheets or towels, with a blue river of paper or fabric running through the landscape. (Base your pictures on the ones on the activity sheet.) Put John the Baptist standing in the water, calling the people to make their lives clean, ready for the coming of the Messiah or Christ. Put in the crowds of people listening to him and deciding to put their lives right. Put some people in the water and move John the Baptist around baptizing them.

There was someone there that day who didn't need to clean up his life at all. It was Jesus. (Put him in.) He came with all the other people because he loved them and wanted to show that he was with them. We don't know what Jesus was praying as he went into the water and was baptized, but we do know that when he had been baptized he was filled with the Holy Spirit. It seemed like a pure white dove flying out of heaven to rest gently on him. (Place the dove just above Jesus.) God's voice was heard from heaven, saying to him, "You are my Son and I love you; I am very pleased with you."

In a way, Jesus was being told his name. He was being told who he was, and what he was called to be during his time on earth.

Praying

Dear Jesus,
you know me even better
than I know myself.
Help me to grow in your Spirit
day by day, all my life through,
rich with the gift of your love. Amen.

Activities

There are instructions on the activity sheet for making a model of the Baptism of Jesus. Each child will need a shoe box, cotton, card, coloring pens and glue.

Notes

What you do

1 Stick on clouds, hills and river to the box.

2 Color and fix on the crowds, Jesus and John the Baptist. Draw other people on hills.

3 Cut out dove and fix with cotton to the top of the box.

Fold and stick on water

Fold and stick on water

Fold under and stick beside water

Fold under and stick on the hillside

How to make a 3D model

You will need

cotton

a shoe box

green paper

shiny blue paper

Cut out

white paper

glue, scissors, colored crayons

To pray this week

Dear Jesus,
You know me even better than I know myself. Help me to grow in your Spirit day by day all my life through, rich with the gifts of your love.   Amen.

Lent

First Sunday of Lent

Thought for the day

Following his baptism, Jesus is severely tempted out in the desert, and shows us how to overcome temptation.

Readings

Deuteronomy 26:4–10
Romans 10:8b–13
Luke 4:1–13

Aim: To know the story of Jesus being tempted and overcoming the temptations.

Starter

Come and sit on my chair. Everyone stands behind a chair except one person who goes out of the room while everyone decides whose chair will be the "correct" one. When the "outsider" comes in, everyone tries to make her sit on their chair, and she chooses a seat. If it is the one agreed upon, the owner of that chair goes outside next. If the wrong chair is chosen she is (very gently) tipped off and can try again. If she gets it wrong three times, someone else goes out and another chair is agreed on.

Teaching

Talk about how we were all tempting our friends to sit on the wrong seat in the game. In real life we are often tempted to do what is wrong, and we sometimes tempt, or encourage, our friends and brothers and sisters to do what is wrong, or avoid doing what is right.

Right after he was baptized, Jesus was badly tempted too, even before his work had properly begun. If he had given in to those temptations, we would not be here today.

First put a large stone down in the center.

Jesus was very hungry. He was fasting, going without food, for forty days, as he talked over with God what his work was, and how it could be done. He knew that he could use God's power. Now he was tempted to use it, not to save people but to change the stones around him into bread so he could eat something.

He knew that would be a wrong way of using God's power. So he said to Satan, "People don't just need real bread to live on—they need my

Father's words to live on as well." Jesus stuck with what was right, so he could go on to feed us with his Father's words of hope and truth.

Now put down a globe.

Satan showed Jesus all the countries of the world, and pretended that he could give them all to him right away, if Jesus would just worship him. Jesus knew that would be completely wrong and that it was a lie, so he told Satan that God is the one you worship, and no one else, no matter what they offer you.

Now put down a first aid box.

Satan suggested that he could win people to him by being a superman, jumping off the top of the temple without being hurt. Satan even quoted from the Bible where it says God's angels will protect you and keep you safe. Jesus said, "Yes, it does say that, and it also says, 'Don't you dare tempt the Lord your God'." Jesus knew that this wasn't the way to get people to follow God. He had to do it by loving them, even if that took longer and meant he would get hurt.

Praying

Jesus, you know what it is like
to be tempted.
And you never gave in.
Please give me the strength
to stand up for what is right. Amen.

Activities

The activity sheet has puzzle activities to reinforce the teaching, and instructions for planting seeds to grow during Lent.

Notes

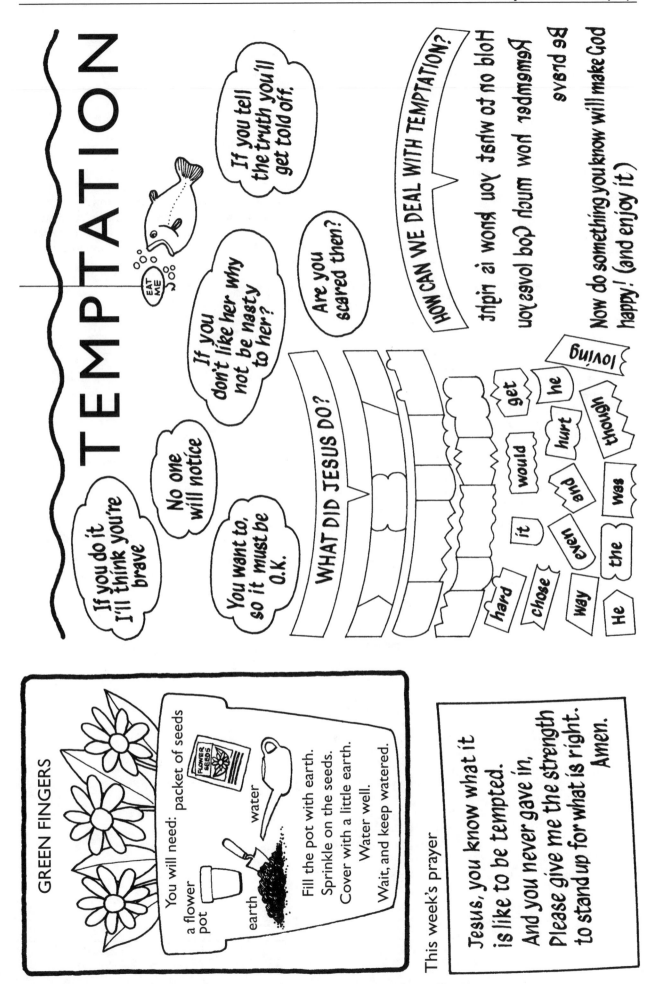

TEMPTATION

If you tell the truth you'll get told off.

EAT ME

If you don't like her why not be nasty to her?

Are you scared then?

If you do it I'll think you're brave

No one will notice

You want to, so it must be O.K.

WHAT DID JESUS DO?

HOW CAN WE DEAL WITH TEMPTATION?

Remember how much God loves you

Hold on to what you know is right

Be brave

Now do something you know will make God happy! (and enjoy it)

He chose the hard way even though it would hurt and he was loving

GREEN FINGERS

You will need: packet of seeds

a flower pot   earth   water

FLOWER SEEDS

Fill the pot with earth.
Sprinkle on the seeds.
Cover with a little earth.
Water well.
Wait, and keep watered.

This week's prayer

Jesus, you know what it is like to be tempted.
And you never gave in.
Please give me the strength to stand up for what is right.
Amen.

Second Sunday of Lent

Thought for the day

God's glory transfigures Jesus as he prays on the mountain. Our lives, too, can become increasingly radiant as the Spirit transforms us.

Readings

Genesis 15:5–12, 17–18
Philippians 3:17—4:1
Luke 9:28–36

Aim: To get to know the events of the Transfiguration.

Starter

Pass the smile; pass the frown. Sit in a circle. Someone starts by smiling at their neighbor who then passes the smile on around the group. When it gets back where it started, try passing the frown around the circle. For a real challenge, start a smile going in one direction and a frown in the other.

Teaching

Point out how the way we behave can get passed on to others. People who are happy often spread that around, and people who are gloomy and bad-tempered spread their gloom. The people who spent time with Jesus on earth were changed by being with him. Today we are going to hear two of those friends talking about a rather strange experience they had with Jesus, something they remembered for the rest of their lives.

Have two of the leaders (or two other volunteers imported for the occasion) be Peter and either James or John. You can have three people if resources run to this. They have just met up and are talking about what happened when they went up the mountain with Jesus and saw him shining as he prayed to his Father. Those who are telling the story need to know the passage very well and talk it through together a couple of times beforehand. Think yourselves into character and talk about it as the real event it was, reminding one another of who you saw there, and what was said, thinking aloud your thoughts about what it meant, and why you were allowed to see it. The children will gain a great sense of immediacy if the conversation is informal but "real."

Have a mirror on the floor with several candles standing on it, and as the disciples get to the point when Jesus is deep in prayer have someone quietly lighting the candles. Nothing needs to be said about this, but the visual alongside the story will help touch their senses with understanding of the wonder of what was being seen.

Praying

Lord Jesus,
in your life we see the glory of God.
In our lives
we want to reflect God's glory
by the way we live.
May our lives
shine with love. Amen.

Activities

On the activity sheet there are instructions for candle decorating. Great care must be taken to ensure everyone's safety. There is also a Bible study activity to reinforce the teaching and a picture to complete of the Transfiguration.

Notes

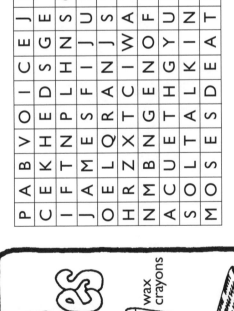

Draw in Jesus on the mountain talking to Moses and Elijah. Make Jesus look as if he is shining.

This week's prayer

Lord Jesus,
in your life
we see the glory of God.
In our lives
we want to reflect God's
glory by the way we live.
May our lives shine with
love.   Amen.

P	A	B	V	O	I	C	E	J	C
C	E	K	H	E	D	S	G	E	L
I	F	T	N	P	L	H	N	S	O
J	A	M	E	S	F	I	J	U	U
O	E	L	Q	R	A	N	J	S	D
H	R	Z	X	T	C	I	W	A	V
N	M	B	N	G	E	N	O	F	H
A	C	U	E	T	H	G	Y	U	K
S	O	L	T	A	L	K	I	N	G
M	O	S	E	S	D	E	A	T	H

JESUS took PETER, JAMES and JOHN up on a MOUNTAIN to pray. As Jesus prayed, his FACE and clothes started SHINING. Then there were two men TALKING with Jesus. They were MOSES and ELIJAH, and they were talking about Jesus' DEATH. Peter wanted it to last for ever. Then a CLOUD came down all around them and they heard God's VOICE saying, 'This is my S_ _, my ch _ _ _ one. Listen to him.' When the voice finished, Jesus was on his own with them again.
Luke 9:28–36

Candles

You will need:
a white candle

wax crayons

a night light in a tin foil dish

old newspapers

WHAT YOU DO

1 Protect your clothes, the table and the floor.

2 Peel the paper off the wax crayons.

3 Melt the end of a crayon and drip the wax onto the candle.

4 Use other colors and cover the candle with colored wax blobs and trickles.

5 Light your candle each day while you pray this week's prayer.

Third Sunday of Lent

Thought for the day

The great "I AM" calls people in every generation to repent so that God's kingdom can be established and grow.

Readings

Exodus 3:1–8, 13–15
1 Corinthians 10:1–6, 10–12
Luke 13:1–9

Aim: To look at the parable of the hopeful gardener and explore its meaning.

Starter

If the location and weather are suitable, take the group out to look at the way some plants are beginning to push shoots up from the earth, and others look like dead twigs but will soon be in bud. Look, too, at which plants seem to be strong and healthy, and which are not thriving at all. If you can't go outside, use house plants and walk around the room as if it's a garden.

Teaching

Back inside, share ideas about the state of all the plants. If they were the gardener, what would they do with the plants which seemed to have given up flowering or fruiting? (No right or wrong answers here.)

Explain that Jesus told a story with a secret meaning (a parable) about a gardener. You will tell them the story Jesus told, and then they can all be detectives and work out what the secret meaning of the story is.

If you can, use a short sound-effects tape of bird song in the country to introduce the reading, and read the passage so it sounds like you are talking, rather than reading it. Then ask everyone these questions:

- Why did the gardener not want to cut the fig tree down right away?

- When are we like the fig tree in this story?

- If it was a thinking and feeling fig tree, what might it think and feel about the gardener?

- What do we learn from this story about the way God feels about us?

Praying

The Lord is compassion and love,
slow to anger and rich in mercy.
For as the heavens are high above the earth

so strong is his love for those who fear him.

(From Psalm 103)

Activities

On the activity sheet they are encouraged to see how God provides us with everything we need to become fruiting trees. They can then check how much they are making use of God's help. They will all need some tracing paper to make the window picture, celebrating God's love and care.

Notes

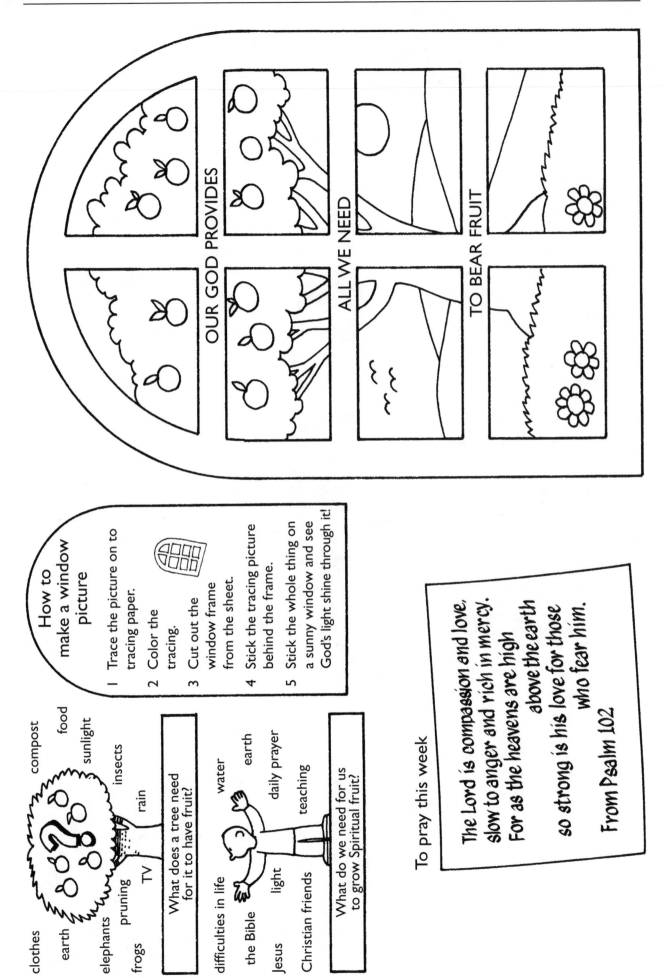

OUR GOD PROVIDES

ALL WE NEED

TO BEAR FRUIT

How to make a window picture

1 Trace the picture on to tracing paper.

2 Color the tracing.

3 Cut out the window frame from the sheet.

4 Stick the tracing picture behind the frame.

5 Stick the whole thing on a sunny window and see God's light shine through it!

compost
food
sunlight
insects
rain

clothes
earth
elephants
pruning
frogs
TV

What does a tree need for it to have fruit?

water
earth
daily prayer
teaching

difficulties in life
the Bible
Jesus
light
Christian friends

What do we need for us to grow Spiritual fruit?

To pray this week

The Lord is compassion and love,
slow to anger and rich in mercy.
For as the heavens are high
above the earth
so strong is his love for those
who fear him.

From Psalm 102

Fourth Sunday
of Lent

Thought for the day

Be reconciled with God. He is waiting to welcome us.

Readings

Joshua 5:9–12
2 Corinthians 5:17–21
Luke 15:1–3, 11–32

Aim: To get to know the parable of the lost son.

Starter

Dear Mr. Crocodile. Mr. Crocodile stands at one end of the room and everyone else at the other end. They all say, "Dear Mr. Crocodile, may we cross your shining river?" Mr. Crocodile then replies, "Only if you're wearing blue or green or yellow or you brushed your teeth this morning or you write with your left hand…" All those in his particular category can take a step forward, and so on. When some of the children reach the other side of the room, they can welcome the next arrivals.

Teaching

Today we are going to hear one of Jesus' stories which is all about a journey home. Choose someone to be the father in the story, and others to be his two grown-up sons. Tell the story from the Bible passage, but using your own words, rather than reading it, so that the children can act it out. The rest of the group join in with all the partying, and they can also be pigs and servants.

After the story, thank all the actors, and ask the children what they think Jesus might want to tell us through this story. Explain that Jesus would often tell stories and then leave everyone to think about them, rather than "decoding" it all for them because he wanted to get them thinking. Invite them to share their ideas about them.

Praying

Father God, when we wander away from you
give us the grace to come to our senses
and start our journey home to your side,
knowing that your arms are open in welcome
because you love us so much.

Activities

Using the activity sheet they can make a model of the son returning to his father. For extra strength, the sheet can be mounted on thin cardboard.

Notes

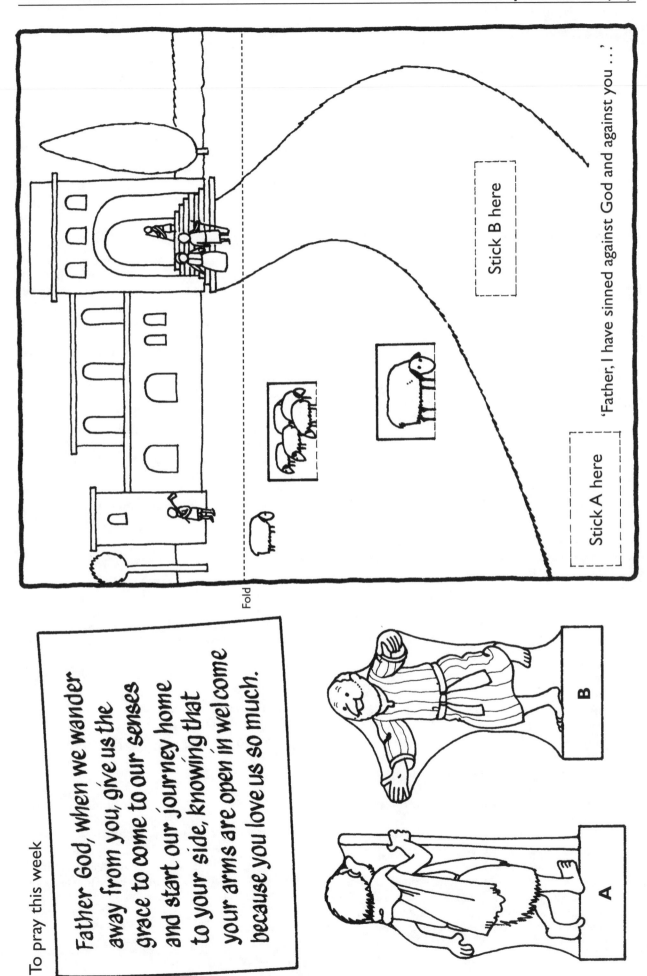

Stick B here

Stick A here

'Father, I have sinned against God and against you . . .'

Fold

To pray this week

Father God, when we wander away from you, give us the grace to come to our senses and start our journey home to your side, knowing that your arms are open in welcome because you love us so much.

A

B

Fifth Sunday
of Lent

Thought for the day

It is not God's wish to condemn anyone, but he longs for us to turn to him and live.

Readings

Isaiah 43:16–21
Philippians 3:8–14
John 8:1–11

Aim: To understand that God does not condemn, but forgives, setting us free.

Starter

Have some wild creatures in a suitable container to look at together. (Snails, worms and beetles, for example.) After talking about them and enjoying them, explain that the creatures aren't able to live freely if we keep them caged up like this, so we need to set them free to enjoy living their lives outside again. Then go out and set the creatures free.

Teaching

Have one of those magic slates and draw someone with a really grumpy expression on it. If we decide that we don't want to have anything to do with such a grumpy picture, we can just slide the slate out and in to clear the screen completely. Now the grumpy picture is wiped away for ever. It's the same with computer screens—we can delete all our mistakes so no one would ever know we'd made them.

Today our readings from the Bible show us that God can do the same kind of thing with us. God doesn't want us to be walking through life weighed down with all our sins so that we can hardly move. God is full of love and mercy, and that means he has the power and authority to forgive us and set us free. Forgiving us is like wiping all our past mistakes and deliberate sins, so that they aren't there anymore. There's an example of Jesus doing this in the gospel today.

(Have a shallow tray of dry earth on the ground in front of you, and a number of rectangular building bricks, or chess pawns which you can place and move around as people.)

To set the event in context, ask everyone what kind of friends Jesus had—were they all good people? No, Jesus was well known for spending his time with people who behaved quite badly, and some of the religious leaders didn't think he should. They thought a good teacher should set a good example by mixing with good, well-behaved people.

One day Jesus was teaching in the temple and a crowd of people were listening to him. (Arrange a crowd of "people.") Suddenly there were shouts and screams, and some other people came in dragging with them a woman who had been caught committing a crime. (Arrange more "people," together with one "person" on their own.) The teachers shouted at Jesus, "Our law says this woman should be stoned to death for committing such a crime—what have you got to say about that?"

Everyone waited to see what Jesus would do. Would he go along with the law and join in the stoning of this criminal? Would he say the sacred law was wrong?

In fact, Jesus didn't say anything. He just bent down and started writing on the dusty ground with his finger. Perhaps he kept rubbing his writing out, as God rubs out our sin. He knew everyone was really steamed-up, and it gave them all some space to cool off and calm down. But they insisted that he should answer them, and eventually Jesus looked up at them (you look up at the faces around you), and said, "Let the person here who has never done anything wrong be the person to throw the first stone."

First of all no one moved. Then the oldest person realized that they had done things that were wrong, and walked quietly away. (Remove one of the "people.") One by one, other people remembered that they weren't perfect either, and moved away (move all the others away), until in the end the woman was left standing there all on her own.

Jesus said to her, "Where are they all—didn't any of them condemn you to death?"

"No one, sir," replied the woman.

Then Jesus looked at her and said, "I don't condemn you either. You're free to go… and don't sin anymore."

So the woman was set free to live. Her crime had been wiped out, and she was given a completely fresh start.

Praying

Lord God, I know that I am not always loving.
Sometimes I am unkind and want my own way.
But I am sorry about this.
Please forgive me and make me more loving.
Amen.

Activities

On the activity sheet there is a picture to color and make into a jigsaw puzzle, so that they can experience the way God mends broken lives and puts people together again when we get messed-up. Mount the picture on card stock before cutting it into pieces, and provide an envelope for each child so they can take their puzzle home with them.

To pray this week

Lord God, I know that
I am not always loving.
Sometimes I am unkind
and want my own way.
But I am sorry about this.
Please forgive me and
make me more loving.
Amen.

God takes the
pieces of broken lives
and puts people
together again

Color,
mount on card, and cut out
pieces, then enjoy putting it
together again

Holy Week

Passion (Palm) Sunday

Thought for the day

As Jesus rides into Jerusalem on a donkey, and the crowds welcome him, we sense both the joy at the Messiah being acclaimed, and the heaviness of his suffering which follows. Jesus' mission is drawing to its fulfillment.

Readings

Liturgy of the Palms:
Luke 19:28–40

Liturgy of the Passion:
Isaiah 50:4–7
Philippians 2:6–11
Luke 22:14—23:56 or Luke 23:1–49

Aim: To get to know the events of Palm Sunday and think about its significance.

Starter

Stop, go, cheer! Make a red "Stop" and a green "Go" sign, and a crown. Have the words for shouting written up large and with a festive feel. When the red sign is shown they have to freeze; when the green sign is shown they can move around the room; and when the crown is shown they shout "Blessed is he who comes in the name of the Lord! Hosanna in the highest!" Sometimes the green sign and the crown can be shown together.

Teaching

The children's classic book *Donkey's Glory* (Nan Goodall) includes the story from the donkey's point of view, and the Palm Tree series includes *Jesus on a Donkey* which tells the story from the point of view of one of the children. Pictures to accompany the telling can be copied on to acetates and shown on an overhead projector, or simply held up and shared.

Praying

Holy, holy, holy, Lord,
God of power and might!
Heaven and earth are full of your glory;
Hosanna in the highest!
Blessed is he who comes in the name of the Lord.
Hosanna in the highest!

Activities

On the activity sheet there are instructions for making a picture in relief using aluminum foil and the template provided. The children may also be joining in with the parish procession, waving streamers, singing and dancing. Another activity on the activity sheet involves decoding a message which can be checked by reading Luke's account of the entry into Jerusalem.

Notes

Palm Sunday

How to make a picture in relief.

You will need:

cooking foil

newspaper

a clip

blunt pencil and a biro

What you do.

Lay the shiny side of the foil on newspaper and the guide picture on top. Draw over the lines and experiment with shading. Keep the papers still.

Code breaker
1, 4, 3, 2,
2, 9, 4, 3,
5, 6, 4, 3,
6, 4, 3, 3

Number of letters in each word

Some of the Pharisees said to Jesus, 'Teacher, tell your followers not to say these things!'

Hosanna! Hosanna!

Peace in heaven and Glory to God!

God bless the King who comes in the name of the Lord!

But Jesus answered,

'It ellyo u,i fmyfo llo wersd on'ts ayt heset hings,t hent hest onesw illc ryout.'

Luke 19 v. 40

Holy, holy, holy, Lord.
God of power and might!
Heaven and earth are full of your glory.
HOSANNA IN THE HIGHEST!
Blessed is he who comes in the name of the Lord.
Hosanna in the highest.

Easter

Easter Day

If possible, it is recommended that the children and young people be in church with the other age groups today. Use and adapt some of the all-age ideas from the *Living Word! Living Water! Complete Resource Book,* and involve the children and young people in some of the music and in the decorating of the church.

Thought for the day

It is true. Jesus is alive for all time. The Lord of life cannot be held by death. God's victory over sin and death means that new life for us is a reality.

Readings

Acts 10:34, 37–43
Colossians 3:1–4
John 20:1–9

Aim: To teach them about the first Easter.

Starter

Have an Easter egg hunt, preferably outside if this is safe and practical.

Teaching

Have two leaders as the women, talking over what happened that morning. It needs to be in a chatty, informal style, rather as two friends might talk over their experience of bumping into someone really famous who helped them pick up the shopping they had dropped. Only this experience of meeting the risen Jesus is so extraordinary that both of them are still fairly dazed by it.

Praying

Christ has died.
Christ has risen.
Christ will come again.
Alleluia!

Activities

On the activity sheet there are instructions for making a cross of flowers. Each child will need a piece of oasis and access to either a garden or a selection of small flowers. There is also a picture of the first Easter morning to complete and color.

Notes

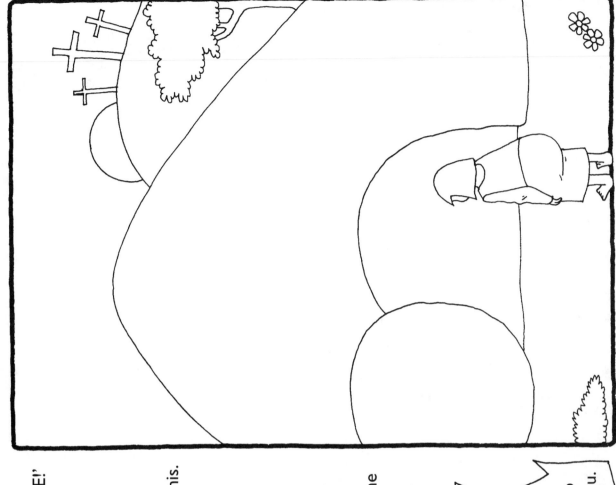

HOW TO MAKE A CROSS WHICH SAYS 'JESUS IS ALIVE!'

What to do:

1 Write the words Jesus is alive on paper.

2 Poke on to the sticks like this.

3 Soak the oasis well.

4 Arrange the flowers and leaves.

5 Fix the sticks in between the flowers.

6 Keep the cross wet.

Can you help the artist finish this picture? Read John 20:1–9 to help you.

You will need:

a cross cut out of oasis

water

some small flowers

3 cocktail sticks

paper, pens and scissors

This week's prayer. Say it as you look at your cross.

Christ has died.
Christ is risen.
Christ will come again.
    Alleluia!

Second Sunday of Easter

Thought for the day

Having seen Jesus in person, the disciples are convinced of the Resurrection. We too can meet him personally.

Readings

Acts 5:12–16
Revelation 1:9–11, 12–13, 17–19
John 20:19–31

Aim: To help them see the reality of Jesus being alive again.

Starter

Play detectives. Everyone stands in a circle with one person in the middle. A ball or balloon is passed around the backs of everyone and the detective in the middle has to discover where the ball is. When they think they know, they point to the person they suspect. If they are right, this person becomes the next detective.

Teaching

Beforehand a leader and a child prepare a short informal conversation in stage whispers, talking together about Peter and the other friends of Jesus, about all the healing that's going on, and the way they are sure that Jesus is very much alive. They are whispering because it's dangerous to be heard talking about Jesus as if he's still alive.

Now Peter (another leader or invited helper) comes in, singing to himself, and the others rush up to him and ask him how he can be so sure that Jesus—who was so completely dead—is completely alive.

Peter explains to them and the children how they know because they've met with Jesus in person. He explains in his own words, and from his own point of view, the events on that first Sunday when Jesus was suddenly there with them, and how he came again the following week, when Thomas was there as well.

Praying

Jesus,
I have heard the witness
of those who saw you alive
after the Resurrection,
and I believe they told the truth.
You are alive,
and I can live my life
in your company!
Thank you, Jesus.

Activities

On the activity sheet there are pictures in speech bubbles so they can pretend they are Peter and Thomas, and some of the healed people, explaining why they know Jesus is really alive. There is also a blank speech bubble for the children to draw in a situation where they know Jesus is really alive (such as receiving communion at Mass; helping them be loving when they want to be nasty; calming their fears).

Notes

This week's prayer

Jesus,
I have heard the witness of those who saw you alive after the resurrection, and I believe they told the truth.
You are alive and I can live my life in your company!
Thank you, Jesus.

Who believed when he had seen Jesus?

Why are these people so sure that Jesus, who was put to death, is alive?

PETER
(John 20:19–20)

I know Jesus is alive because …

I know Jesus is alive because …

THOMAS
(John 20:24–28)

A HEALED PERSON
(Acts 5:14–16)

I know Jesus is alive because …

I know Jesus is alive because …

YOU!

This is what you saw. Look at it for a minute, then cover it up.
Now you are called to be a witness

How many people were robbing the bank?

What were they wearing?

Did you see anyone holding a gun?

You

You

You

Witnesses are very important

Third Sunday of Easter

Thought for the day

Those who know Jesus and recognize that he is the anointed Savior are commissioned to go out as his witnesses to proclaim the good news.

Readings

Acts 5:27–32, 40–41
Revelation 5:11–14
John 21:1–19

Aim: For them to connect Peter's previous denial with today's commitment and commissioning.

Starter

Sit in a circle and go on a campfire-style "lion hunt." The journey to the cave—through short grass, long grass, sticky mud, water and so on—is repeated at speed in the other direction on the return journey. Today we're going to look at the way we sometimes have to go back the way we came to put things right in our lives.

Teaching

Have a fishing net (such as a net curtain), some shiny paper fish, some driftwood and matches, and a mirror, explaining that all these come into today's story. Read the story from the *International Children's Version* or the *Good News Bible*, asking the children to listen for when the objects are mentioned. This will help to focus their listening, and they will also notice that the matches are there as a sign of the driftwood being a fire, and there is no mention of a mirror. Explain that the mirror is, like the matches, a sign for something that is going on in the story.

Show people their faces in the mirror and point out that by doing this you are helping them to see for themselves what they look like. In our story Jesus is helping Peter to see what he is really like, and in our lives Jesus helps each of us to see what we are like as people. Some things we know already. You probably know if you are a kind person, or if you worry a lot, or if you get easily upset, or if everything makes you laugh. You might already know whether you are good or bad at telling the truth, making up quickly after an argument, or cheering up your friends. That's good. Jesus wants us to get to know ourselves.

Sometimes people get frightened by what they find out about themselves. Perhaps they would like to think they were kind, but they find out that really they are quite unkind. Peter wanted to be the kind of person who would stick up for Jesus however

dangerous it became, but he found out on Good Friday that he was actually a bit of a coward. Three times he had denied he even knew Jesus.

Jesus wanted to show him that he still loved him, and it was OK to be like he really was, so long as he didn't pretend he was different. That way Jesus could help him learn to be the brave person he wanted to be. Three times Jesus gave Peter the chance to say he loved him, so that the past was put right.

And Jesus says to us, "It's OK to be the person you are. You don't need to pretend you're different. Together we can work on the things you find hard."

Praying

Jesus, you're right.
There isn't any point in pretending with you,
because you know me as I really am.
I'm glad I'm me, if you're glad I'm me!
Let's work together
on those things I find hard. Amen.

Activities

The separate figures on the activity sheet can be colored and cut out and stuck on to a background of blue and yellow posterboard. Other things can be added, such as pieces of net and shiny fish, to create a collage picture. There is also an activity on the sheet to link Peter's denial with this fresh chance to put things right.

Notes

The problem

Peter said:

You speak like him – you must be with him!

Peter said:

Aren't you one of his gang?

Peter said:

I saw you with him, didn't I?

Look how Jesus sorted it out

Do you love me, Simon?

Peter said:

Do you love me, Simon?

Peter said:

Do you love me, Simon?

Peter said:

Color and cut out these pictures and mount them on a background of sky, sand and sea. Add woolly clouds, shiny fish and a sun.

This week's prayer

Jesus, you're right.
There isn't any point in pretending with you, because you know me as I really am.
I'm glad I'm me, if you're glad I'm me!
Let's work together on those things I find hard.
       Amen.

Fourth Sunday of Easter

Thought for the day

Jesus, the Good Shepherd, leads his flock into eternal life.

Readings

Acts 13:14, 43–52
Revelation 7:9, 14–17
John 10:27–30

Aim: To know that Jesus is the Good Shepherd whom they can trust to lead them.

Starter

Play "follow the leader," with the leader pretending to be different animals in turn. Everyone else copies the leader. Swap leaders a few times and accompany the game with a praise tape.

Teaching

Beforehand record a few voices which are well known to the children. Some are famous people, and others are local, familiar voices, such as the priest, a teacher at school, or a parent. Play the voice recordings, one at a time, and see if the children recognize them. Explain that today we are going to look at something Jesus said about recognizing voices.

How did they recognize the voices on tape? Because they were used to hearing those people—they knew what their voices sounded like, even if they hadn't heard them saying those words before.

Ask them to listen out for the answer to this question: "Who recognizes the Good Shepherd's voice?" as you read them today's gospel. Read it slowly and clearly, with short pauses between the phrases to help them take in the meaning. (The answer to the question is the sheep that belong to the Good Shepherd.) Who is the Good Shepherd? Jesus. And who are the sheep who belong to him and recognize his voice? Those who follow Jesus—people like us! Just as a good shepherd leads and guides all his sheep and lambs and keeps them safe, Jesus, our Good Shepherd, leads and guides us safely through all the dangers and evils all the days of our life and, when we eventually die, he goes on leading us safely to heaven.

Praying

Jesus, our Good Shepherd,
when you call us, we will follow,
where you lead us, we will go,
because we know your voice of love
will lead us safely
all the way to heaven. Amen.

Activities

On the activity sheet there is a game to make and play, where they only obey the instructions given by the shepherd. For counters the children make a small model sheep from playdough, or they can cut out the sheep pictured.

Notes

Only obey the shepherd!

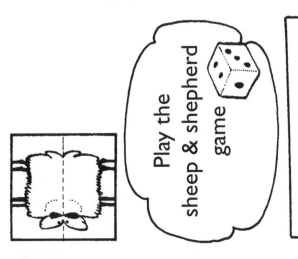

Play the
sheep & shepherd
game

Jesus,
our Good Shepherd,
when you call us, we
will follow, where you
lead us, we will go,
because we know your
voice of love will lead
us safely all the way
to heaven.   Amen.

Fifth Sunday of Easter

Thought for the day
Christ, breaking through the barrier of sin and death, allows us to break into an entirely new way of living which continues into eternity.

Readings
Acts 14:21–27
Revelation 21:1–5
John 13:31–35

Aim: To explore the nature of friendship and what it means to be God's friend.

Starter
If you can borrow a parachute, some parachute games would be excellent, as they help develop the qualities of sharing and cooperation. Alternatively play some circle games, such as passing the smile or passing the hand squeeze, and place-changing. (In this everyone makes a drum roll with hands on thighs, and chants, "Is it you, is it me, who will it be? Who will it be?" Then the leader calls out the category, such as those who ate Sugar Puffs for breakfast, those who are wearing stripes, or those who have a sister, and these people get up and change places.

Teaching
Explain that Jesus told his disciples they were to love one another. The way other people will recognize that we are Jesus' friends is by the way we love one another. If we don't live like that, it really means we are not his friends. Who do you think can be one of Jesus' friends? Is it only those brought up to go to church? Or only the ones who don't have bad tempers? Or only the ones who can read the Bible? (They can think about this; we'll talk about it after the story.)

Tell the story from the Early Church of how Paul and Barnabas had to make new friends in new places, and how people had to recognize that they were Jesus' friends.

After the story, go back to the question you left the children to think about, and in a circle, so that all have a chance to speak, share their ideas.

Praying
Jesus, you are my friend
as well as my Lord and Savior.
Please teach me to be a good friend
to others
all my life. Amen.

Activities
On the activity sheet the children are encouraged to look at the qualities of a good friend, and I have included several things which may or may not be considered necessary, as well as some obvious choices. It is valuable for children of this age to start looking at the values they are living by, so that they learn to make thoughtful choices in the way they live.

Notes

Jesus said, 'You are my friends, if . . .

WHY OUT AOW LET
RA WO THE TRED
BOY O JU EL

John 13.34

How to show people what a good friend Jesus is.

Draw and color your ideas on circles of paper.

Your life can show people what Jesus is like

Stick the ideas on a cross shape made of wallpaper.

Show the cross in the hall or at your school or in the library.

Am I a good friend?

What makes a good friend?

They support the same team

They listen to what you say

They stick up for you

They help you

They won't tell your secrets to anyone else

They are less clever than you

They tell you what to do and which music to like

They make you feel happy

They think you're nice

They don't let you down

They like the same music

They don't boss you around

They are fun to be with

They like you unless other people are there

They buy you expensive presents

They tell you if you've upset them

Put a ring round the things that make a good friend

This week's prayer

Jesus, you are my friend as well as my Lord and Saviour. Please teach me to be a good friend to others all my life.   Amen.

Sixth Sunday
of Easter

Thought for the day

The continuing presence of God, as Holy Spirit, leads us, as Jesus promised, into a personally guided outreach to all nations.

Readings

Acts 15:1–2, 22–29
Revelation 21:10–14, 22–23
John 14:23–29

Aim: To look at God's provision for us in the leading and guidance of the Holy Spirit.

Starter

Pair the children up and blindfold one of the pair. They take turns leading the blindfolded one around the grounds, taking great care to protect each other from danger.

Teaching

Talk over how it felt to be unable to see, and how it helped to have a friend to help us travel safely. When Jesus was with his friends at the last supper he talked to them about having to leave them. They were very sad and rather anxious at the thought of living without their good and wise friend there in person. Jesus had always been able to sort out their fears, cheer them up, get them to make up after arguments, and point out the right things to do. How on earth would they be able to cope without him? And how would they be brave enough to tell other people about him when they knew that would put them in danger?

Read the gospel for today, asking them to listen for a promise Jesus gave. They can put their hands up when they hear it, and John 14:23 can be displayed for everyone to read together. So the disciples (and that includes us) were not going to be left like orphans to manage on their own. Somehow God would be with them, in a real and personal way, even though it wouldn't be a person they could see physically.

To get just one idea of how this worked out, tell the children about a time after the Resurrection, when Paul and his friends were travelling around telling people about the God of love. Tell them how the Spirit stopped them going to some places they planned, and led them straight to another place, where some people were ready to hear the good news and become Christians. All over the world, and in each century, God the Holy Spirit is there, guiding people to understand God's will and open doors and nudge in the right direction.

Praying

You could sing *Waiting for your Spirit* by Mick Gisbey, and have this prayer during the music interlude between verses:

Lord, I want to go wherever you need me.
Train me to notice
your quiet voice
showing me
the right way to live. Amen.

Activities

There is a short quiz and drawing activity on the activity sheet to get the children thinking about the way loving involves taking thought and care for people. This may be an opportunity to recognize that rules their parents make may sometimes seem a pain but really they show that our parents care about us. There is also an opening to learn the need to listen to God's Spirit, and to practice this during the week. If there is time the children can color some flags of different countries with the words "God loves you" written in the appropriate language. These can be laid on the floor around the altar for people to see as they gather for communion.

Here are some languages to start you off:

French:	Dieu vous aime
German:	Gott liebt dich
Italian:	Dio ti ama
Spanish:	Dios te ama
Swahili:	Mungu anakupenda

Notes

Jesus says goodbye

(and gives a promise)
John 14:23

Put these in order

a Boeing 747 taking off beside you (e)

your mom singing in the bath (d)

bacon frying (c)

a piano being dropped downstairs (b)

a pin dropping on a carpet (a)

VERY LOUD

ff

very quiet

pp

To pray this week

Lord, I want to go wherever you need me. Train me to notice your quiet voice showing me the right way to live.
Amen.

God's guiding Spirit is often very quiet – we need to listen carefully

What happens next?   Draw it here

When your parents say goodbye to you, do they

☐ leave you on your own for a week

☐ make sure there's someone to look after you

If your babysitter is looking after you does he/she

☐ let you play ball on a busy road

☐ make sure you and your friends are safe

pe○ple us l○○k us The l○ve④ who after

Write it out in the right order.
The fourth word is done for you.

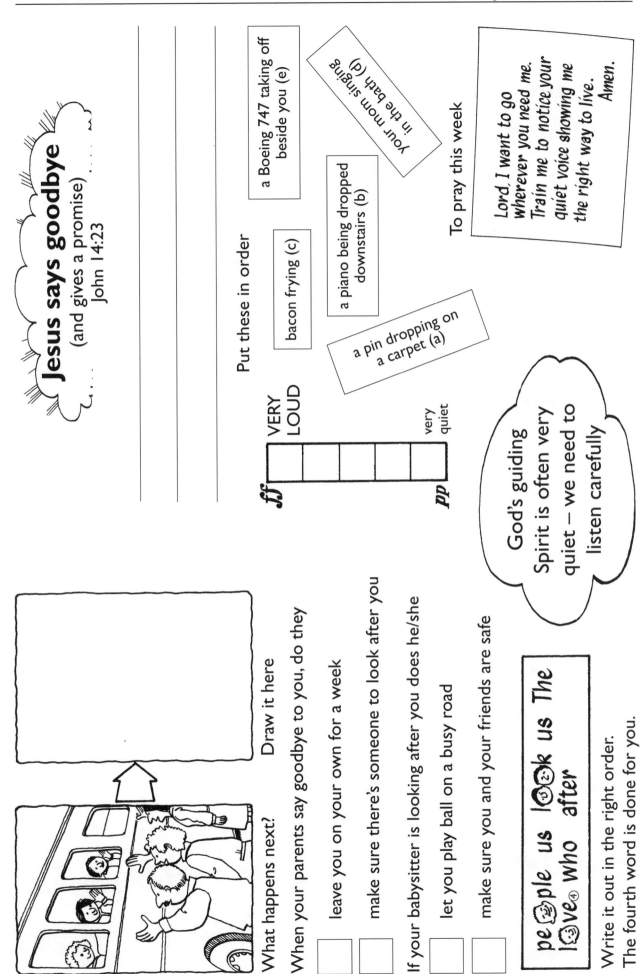

The Ascension
of the Lord

Thought for the day

Having bought back our freedom with the giving of his life, Jesus enters into the full glory to which he is entitled.

Readings

Acts 1:1–11
Ephesians 1:17–23
Luke 24:46–53

Activities

It is likely that Ascension Day services for schools will not need a separate program for children and young people. However, I have included a drawing and coloring activity for today.

You may also like to consider using some of the All-age ideas from the Complete Resource Book.

- Any artwork or writing that the children have done on what the Ascension is about can be displayed around the building.

- Have a beautiful helium balloon ready. Write on it an Ascension message that the children would like to send. After the service two representative children can let the balloon float away.

- Children can wave white and yellow streamers during some of the hymns.

Notes

Seventh Sunday of Easter

Thought for the day

Jesus lives for all time in glory; we can live the fullness of Resurrection life right away.

Readings

Acts 7:55–60
Revelation 22:12–14, 16–17, 20
John 17:20–26

Aim: To see the new life in action, through Stephen's story.

Starter

Sitting in a circle, pass around a trophy type of cup. As each person holds it they name something they are able to do. Everyone responds, "Thank you, God, for making us!" We are all equipped for whatever God wants us to do, and the gifts we are given are there to be used in the very best way.

Teaching

Remind the children that we have just celebrated Ascension Day. Tell them about this last time the disciples met with Jesus, what he said to them, and where he was going. On a calendar they can work out how long Jesus had been around in his risen state since the Resurrection.

Today we are going to see an example of the kind of life Jesus' followers were living after Jesus had returned to heaven, and the Holy Spirit had been sent to equip the disciples for God's work.

Introduce an invited guest (one of the leaders dressed up) to tell everyone his story. He is holding a stone, which he fingers as he talks. He tells them how Stephen was one of those followers of the man Jesus who had been executed by crucifixion, but these followers of his were convinced he had come back to life, and was the promised Messiah. The teller had tried his best to stamp out this group of people—known as "followers of the Way." How could this Jesus be the Son of God? How could the Son of God end up dying a cursed death on a Roman cross?

He explains how Stephen had something about him which did seem to point to him speaking the truth, and he had worked hard to prove his claims about Jesus from Scripture, but it just wasn't right for these Jesus-followers to be going about happy as if Jesus really was alive and had power to live in them.

He explains how he had joined the others with stones to throw at Stephen and put him to death, but something had stopped him throwing his stone. It was the way Stephen had stood there, with stones hitting him, and gazed up into heaven as if he really could see into it. And as the stones knocked him to his knees, Stephen was actually praying for God to forgive those of us killing him! He describes how Stephen's example has made him think again about Jesus, and he's decided to find out more about being a follower of the Way. He's going to keep the stone he nearly threw to remind him.

Praying

Thank you, Jesus,
for the new life
you have won for me.
Fill me up
with the Spirit of God
so that I can live life
to the full. Amen.

Activities

The activity sheet reinforces the teaching with space for them to draw in what Stephen could see. They will need a Bible for this. There is also a question about the quality and direction of their own lives to think over, either in small groups or on their own during the week.

Notes

Cut these shapes out carefully and arrange them on the black patch to make the answer to the question.

Draw in what Stephen could see (Acts 7:55–60)

What is most important to me in life?

"I can see thrown of Man the and the Son at of God!"

Look up John 17:20

Q. Who was Jesus praying for?

A. He was praying for

EHT SISCDILPE

and for

To pray this week

Thank you, Jesus for the new life you have won for me. Fill me up with the Spirit of God so I can live life to the full.   Amen.

Pentecost

Thought for the day

As Jesus promised, the Holy Spirit is poured out on the apostles and the Church is born.

Readings

Acts 2:1–11
1 Corinthians 12:3–7, 12–13
John 20:19–23

Aim: To become familiar with the events at Pentecost.

Starter

Play a game where the children are waiting expectantly but can only act when they hear the instruction. Here is one example. Everyone finds a space to stand in and the leader calls "One...two...three hop to the window/crawl like snakes/pirouette around the table/score the winning goal." (Choose a variety of activities to suit your group.)

Teaching

Remind the children of how, at the Ascension, the disciples had been told by Jesus to wait in Jerusalem for the gift of the Holy Spirit to come. They went back and spent time praying together so they would be ready for the Spirit when it came.

Have some of the children be the apostles, waiting and praying together. As you read or tell them about the way the Spirit came, the other children can make the sound of an orchestrated rushing wind, and some can be given red crepe paper streamers to whirl around the place where the apostles are sitting. As the wind dies away and the disciples are left alone, tell the children how the Spirit had made them full of excitement and joy. They were longing to tell everyone about Jesus, and the way God loves us.

The apostles can now come running and dancing out to the crowd in the street, telling them that Jesus of Nazareth, who had been crucified, was the promised Messiah, the Christ, the Son of God. End with the people asking to be baptized and to become his followers.

Praying

Fill my life,
Holy Spirit of God,
with joy and love and hope.
Live in me so I can show others
how much you love them. Amen.

Activities

Using the template on the activity sheet the children can cut out lots of flames in red, yellow and orange. These can be given out to the rest of the congregation after the service. There is also a Pentecost wordsearch to reinforce the teaching. Finding words from Pentecost will also help to familiarize them with this word.

Notes

Cut out flame shapes from red, yellow and orange paper. Cut out the messages. Stick them on the flames. Give them to people and pray for those you give them to.

H	O	L	Y	S	P	I	R	I	T
A	P	P	E	C	F	W	R	A	X
J	U	E	H	S	L	B	F	P	N
F	I	A	N	G	A	D	O	O	M
Z	J	C	B	T	M	W	L	S	H
T	A	E	Z	Q	E	I	W	T	R
P	M	R	D	R	D	C	J	L	Y
G	S	N	P	L	O	K	O	E	N
O	I	V	E	T	C	V	Y	S	K
W	Y	U	X	L	O	V	E	Q	T

PENTECOST   APOSTLES
HOLY SPIRIT   POWER
LOVE   JOY   PEACE
WIND   FLAME

God loves you

Jesus is still alive

Seek and you will find

Come, Holy Spirit!

The Spirit gives life

The Spirit brings freedom

God's Spirit be with you

May God's love surround you

Ask and you will receive

Love, Joy, Peace

Let the Spirit of God enfold you

Holy Spirit, flood into my whole life!

Fill my life, Holy Spirit of God, with joy and love and hope. *Live in me* so I can show others how much you love them.   *Amen.*

Feasts of the Lord

Trinity Sunday

Thought for the day

The unique nature of God is celebrated today, as we reflect on the truth that God is Creator, Redeemer and Life-giver.

Readings

Proverbs 8:22–31
Romans 5:1–5
John 16:12–15

Aim: To understand more about the nature of God.

Starter

Set out different colors of paints and help them to do color sums, like this:

Red + Yellow =
Yellow + Blue =
Red + Green =

Teaching

Beforehand prepare the word "Trinity" on two pieces of card, with "Tri" on one piece and "Unity" on the other.

First look together at the color sums, and point out the way that although we put clear yellow and clear blue in, you can't see them anymore once they've turned green. They have become something different.

Today is called Trinity Sunday, and we're going to look at what that means. Show the cards as "Trinity." Then put the "Unity" card down and concentrate on the "Tri." Talk about words they know which have this in them, such as tricycle, tripod and triangle. Between you figure out from these words what TRI means. What does three have to do with God? Draw three dots on a sheet of paper and name them with their help, God the Father, God the Son and God the Holy Spirit.

Now pick up the "Unity" section. Block off the "y" and ask what words they know with "unit" in them, such as united, unit, and unite. If anyone can count in French you can ask them what "un" means in French. Figure out together the meaning of "Unity." What does this have to do with God? Draw lines joining the three dots together to form a triangle and explain that there is only one God. But unlike the colors we made, we can still see the three different "colors" of God in his nature. That's why the Church has squashed the two words "Tri" and "Unity" together, to make a word that tries to understand God better. Join the two pieces of cards together again, and put the word next to the drawing.

Praying

Glory be to God the Father,
Glory be to God the Son,
Glory be to God the Spirit,
Holy Trinity, three in one!

Activities

There are instructions on the activity sheet for making a Trinity bookmark using clover leaves and sticky-backed plastic. An alternative method is to use clover-leaf shapes cut from green paper. There are some other puzzles to solve, and a story of Patrick and the child on the beach.

Notes

TRINITY

Tell your family what it means.

Saint Patrick was on the beach trying to understand the Trinity. He watched a child trying to fill a hole in the sand with sea water. Patrick went over to him. 'You'll never manage that, you know,' he said. 'The water will keep draining away.' The child replied, 'And neither will you ever manage to understand the Trinity.'

TRINITY

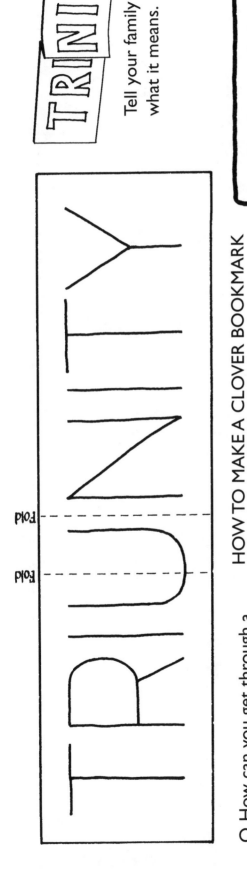

- - - Fold

- - - Fold

HOW TO MAKE A CLOVER BOOKMARK

You will need

colored card and scissors

a clothespin

clover

sticky backed plastic

What you do
Cut this shape from card. Stick clover leaves on it. Cover with plastic. Stick to the clothespin.

Q How can you get through a sheet of paper?

A Cut it like this:

Here

and here

To pray this week

Glory be to God the Father.
Glory be to God the Son.
Glory be to God the Spirit.
Holy Trinity, 3 in 1!

Corpus Christi

Thought for the day

Jesus is the Living Bread, who brings us eternal life through Communion with him.

Readings

Genesis 14:18–20
1 Corinthians 11:23–26
Luke 9:11–17

Activities

It is likely that Corpus Christi services for schools will not need a separate program for children and young people. However, I have included an activity sheet for children in church today.

Notes

To pray today

Lord Jesus, you are the Bread of Life. Whoever feeds on this bread will never go hungry.

Can you spot: Jesus ☐   Some bread ☐   some fish ☐

a basket ☐   God's loving kindness ☐

Ordinary Time

Second Sunday in Ordinary Time

Thought for the day

As a marriage celebrates the beginning of a changed, new life for the bride and groom, so our loving, faithful God has chosen us and is ready to transform our lives for the good of the world.

Readings

Isaiah 62:1–5
1 Corinthians 12:4–11
John 2:1–11

Aim: To see the wedding at Cana as a sign of God's glory shown in Jesus.

Starter

A tasting survey. Have a number of different fruit drinks and some drinking cups. Blindfold some volunteers and give them the different drinks to taste, asking them to name them. Record their opinions on a chart and then let them take off the blindfold and reveal the identity of the drinks.

Teaching

Explain how we are going to hear about some people whose drink gave them a rather nice surprise. Have one of the servants telling the story. S/he can be holding a water jar and wearing appropriate clothing or headcovering to add to the effect. Whoever is telling the story needs to know the events well, and see it all from the servant's point of view. You can then slip in bits of hearsay about this man, Jesus, and comment on how you felt as he told you what to say and what it was that made you prepared to go along with what he told you to do. The aim is to help the children see what happened as if they were there as well.

Remind the children of the meaning of the Epiphany, and talk with them about what was being shown about God in this event. Read what John says at the end of his account. They had already decided to follow, and this sign backed up their decision.

Praying

Fill us up to the brim
with your Spirit, O Lord,
> *(with hands horizontal like a water level, raise the level to the top of your head)*

and use our lives
> *(open up hands and extend them in offering)*

for the good of the world.
> *(trace large circle in the air with hands)*

Amen.

Activities

The teaching is reinforced on the activity sheet with an activity which matches different people with different reactions. There is also space to record discussion outcomes concerning the significance of this event. Instructions are included for making a "black-and-white into color" picture.

Notes

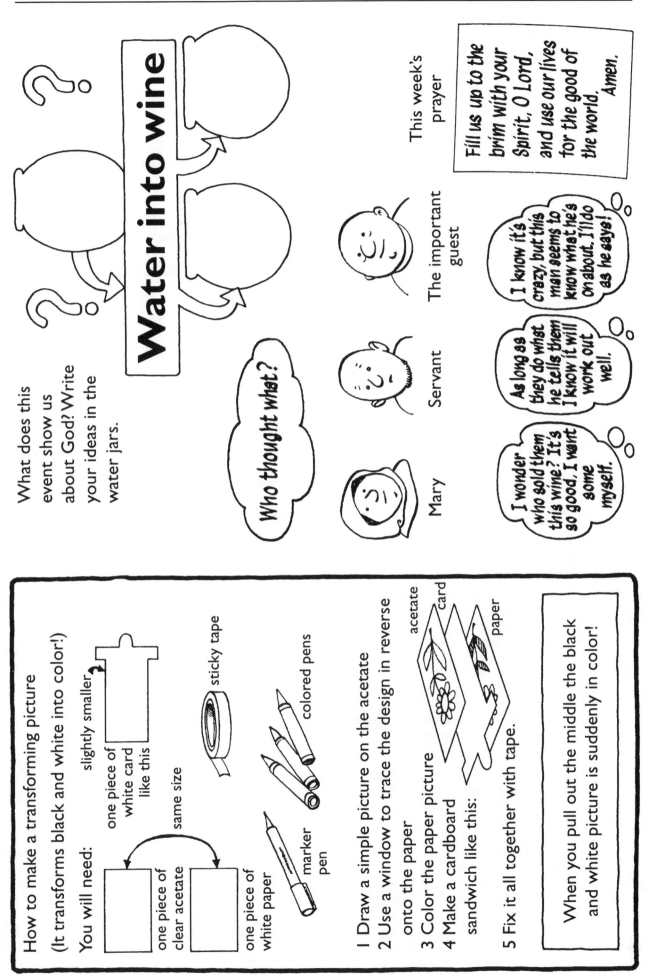

Water into wine

What does this event show us about God? Write your ideas in the water jars.

Who thought what?

Mary

Servant

The important guest

I wonder who sold them this wine? It's so good, I want some myself.

As long as they do what he tells them I know it will work out well.

I know it's crazy, but this man seems to know what he's on about. I'll do as he says!

This week's prayer

Fill us up to the brim with your Spirit, O Lord, and use our lives for the good of the world. Amen.

How to make a transforming picture
(It transforms black and white into color!)

You will need:

one piece of clear acetate

one piece of white card like this

same size

slightly smaller

one piece of white paper

marker pen

colored pens

sticky tape

1 Draw a simple picture on the acetate
2 Use a window to trace the design in reverse onto the paper
3 Color the paper picture
4 Make a cardboard sandwich like this:

acetate

card

paper

5 Fix it all together with tape.

When you pull out the middle the black and white picture is suddenly in color!

Third Sunday in Ordinary Time

Thought for the day

The meaning of the Scriptures is revealed to the people.

Readings

Nehemiah 8:2–6, 8–10
1 Corinthians 12:12–30
Luke 1:1–4; 4:14–21

Aim: To see how God is revealed through the Scriptures.

Starter

Who can it be? Sit in a circle. Start giving one piece of information about a particular child and continue down the clues until someone guesses who you are describing.

Teaching

Point out how in the game the words that were spoken gave everyone clues about the person being described. No one has ever seen God in this life, but we have been given plenty of good clues in the writings in the Bible. Look together at the passage from Isaiah. Who do they think it sounds like it is describing? It does sound very much like Jesus because he did those things in his life.

This prophecy of Isaiah was well known to the people in the town of Nazareth, where Jesus grew up. But at that time they had no idea who the prophet was talking about. They were in for quite a surprise one morning when they went to worship at their local synagogue.

Now act out the gospel for today much as described in the All-age ideas, involving an attendant who gives you the scroll to read from. Make yourself thoroughly familiar with the text beforehand so that the other parts of the gospel can be told informally. Have the words of the chorus to "God's Spirit is in my heart" displayed so that they can be read or sung afterwards:

> He sent me to give the Good News to the poor
> tell pris'ners that they are pris'ners no more,
> tell blind people that they can see
> and set the downtrodden free,
> and go tell ev'ryone
> the news that the kingdom of God has come
> and go tell ev'ryone
> the news that God's kingdom has come.

Talk together about how they might have felt if they had been there that morning and record their ideas on a sheet of paper headed: "When Jesus preached this week I wondered/felt/thought …." Then you can write their thoughts in thought bubbles.

Praying

Jesus, I know you always speak what is true.
Help me to listen
with my heart as well as my ears. Amen.

Activities

Make a group collage of today's gospel, based on the picture drawn below.

Give the children the appropriate sized pieces of paper to draw various people from the town and clothe them by cutting and sticking from a selection of different colored and textured paper or fabric. All the characters are then assembled in the synagogue and Jesus can be holding a rolled scroll. The title for the collage is "Today this Scripture is fulfilled in your hearing."

The activity sheet looks at our need to listen so that when God is speaking to us through his word we are able to hear him.

Notes

Draw a person for a synagogue collage

This week's prayer

Jesus,
I know you always speak what is true.
Help me to listen with my heart as well as my ears.
Amen.

What might you pretend *not* to hear
Mom say? (next time, listen and hear!)

How loud?

Mark it on the scale

We can hear some things easily.
To hear others we have to listen
very carefully.

When do we need to listen
to what God is saying?

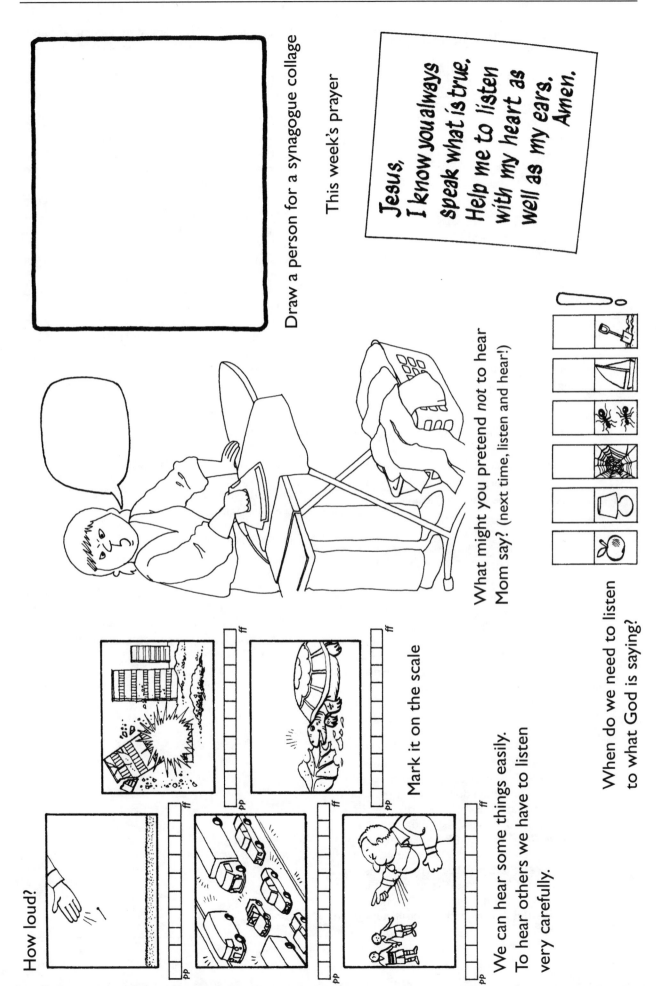

Fourth Sunday in Ordinary Time

Thought for the day

As a prophet, Jesus' work is to proclaim the reign of God's love, not only to the Jewish people but to the whole world.

Readings

Jeremiah 1:4–5, 17–19
1 Corinthians 12:31—13:13
Luke 4:21–30

Aim: To know the events of today's gospel.

Starter

Riddles. Split into teams, give each team a bell or horn, and ask some riddles. The first team to ring their bell and give the right answer gains a point. The winning team has a small prize. Choose riddles which you solve by looking at the question in a different way, like these:

• What has four wheels and flies? A garbage truck.
• When is a door not a door? When it's ajar.
• What goes up when it comes down? An umbrella.
• What runs but cannot walk? Water.

Teaching

Those riddles only made sense once we started understanding them in a new way. Until then, they sounded like nonsense—to run yet not be able to walk; to be a door and yet not to be a door. Today we are going to find that Jesus is a rather like a riddle for the people in his hometown to solve.

Two leaders or imported Adventurers stand up and start a "Have you heard about the miracles of healing Jesus has been doing?" conversation together about some of the healings they've heard about. They finish by saying they can't wait to see what happens when he comes home to Nazareth. Then they sit down.

Explain that Jesus came that weekend to his hometown of Nazareth, and that Sabbath everyone crowded into the synagogue to hear him, and see what miracles he would do for them. Perhaps they were fed up that he hadn't started at his hometown. They liked it when he told them the old prophecies were being fulfilled today, in their own synagogue. They all waited for some amazing signs and wonders to happen because that was what they were expecting Jesus to do. As his hometown, they thought he ought to make it extra special.

But Jesus didn't do anything spectacular at all.

Instead he told them they were looking at him in the wrong way, and didn't understand what he was there for. Jesus wasn't there to do clever tricks, but to show God's love. If they could only see him as a local boy doing clever tricks, then they wouldn't get to see any of the wonderful signs of God's love! He even hinted that there were plenty of outsiders who would end up seeing more than they.

The two leaders or Adventurers stand up again, talking angrily about the way Jesus had upset them that day, and how disappointed they were in him, even if he was a local lad. They remind each other of the way the men in their town had dragged Jesus out of the synagogue and thrown him out of the town. They end up folding their arms and both agreeing that it was disgraceful! Then they sit down.

What had Jesus done wrong? Nothing, except to tell them the truth, which they didn't want to hear. It wouldn't have helped them get to know God better if Jesus had done what they wanted and performed lots of miracles. Miracles are not magic tricks, and Jesus wasn't a clever magician. If the people didn't trust in God's love, they wouldn't be able to see it in action anyway. And neither will we.

Praying

Father God,
train us to want what you want;
to see as you see
and understand as you do.
Let your kingdom come and
your will be done on earth
as it is in heaven. Amen.

Activities

The activity sheet can be made into a model of the people angrily forcing Jesus out of the synagogue. They are also encouraged to think about times we try to push Jesus away because we don't want to hear what he is saying in our hearts.

Notes

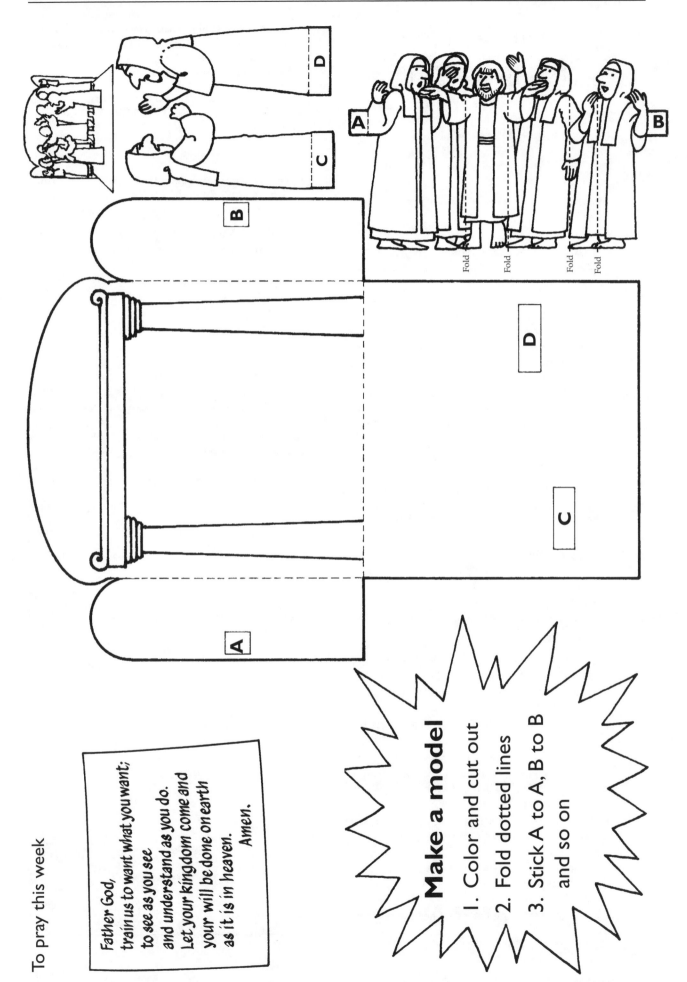

To pray this week

Father God,
train us to want what you want;
to see as you see
and understand as you do.
Let your kingdom come and
your will be done on earth
as it is in heaven.
Amen.

Make a model

1. Color and cut out
2. Fold dotted lines
3. Stick A to A, B to B and so on

Fifth Sunday in Ordinary Time

Thought for the day
God calls his people and commissions them.

Readings
Isaiah 6:1–8
1 Corinthians 15:1–11
Luke 5:1–11

Aim: To see the stages that Simon Peter went through in this calling.

Starter
Pass it on. Sit in a circle and choose a leader. The leader does something (claps hands, crosses legs, winks, etc.) and this action is taken up by each person one by one, going clockwise around the circle. When it gets back to the leader, they start a new action for the next round. The point is that each person needs to be attentive to what the person sitting next to them is doing, and they then become the next in the chain of passing the message on.

Teaching
Beforehand prepare a film clapperboard to snap shut as signs with the following headings are displayed. (The titles in parentheses are written on the reverse.)
1. The night shift
2. Simon helps out *(welcome Jesus)*
3. Time to listen *(listen to him)*
4. The Maker's instructions *(see him in action)*
5. I'm not good enough! *(recognize who he is)*
6. Follow me *(follow him)*

Go through the story as if the film is being made, narrating it, with the leaders and children acting it out.
1. The children act the setting out and pulling in of empty nets through the night.
2. The crowd arrives, and Simon Peter offers Jesus his boat to sit in.
3. Simon Peter sits on the sand with the crowd, first busy with his nets and gradually listening more attentively. Give out an old piece of netting for everyone to work on.
4. Jesus tells the fishermen to cast their nets again and they do so, with surprising and dramatic results.
5. Simon Peter reacts to the huge catch by realizing Jesus' importance and his own lack of goodness.
6. Jesus shows Simon Peter that he knows what he

is like and still wants him to work for the spreading of the kingdom of God. He calls him to follow and search for people instead of fish. Simon Peter follows him.

Display all the signs in order, then turn them over to show the titles in brackets. These lead on to the prayer time.

Praying
Give the children a set of five paper footprints, which they put down in a line in front of them. As you pray, move forward to each footprint in turn:

Like Simon Peter
I want to *welcome* you, Jesus,
listen to what you say,
see what you do,
get to *know* you better
and *follow* you all my life. Amen.

Activities
On the activity sheet there are instructions for making a fishes-and-shell mobile, based on today's prayer. You will need to have string, card, and a shell for each child. There is also a wordsearch to reinforce the teaching, and a picture to complete, which will give them the sense of things falling into place as Jesus enables us to see where we need to go next in life.

Notes

Word Search

F	A	J	O	T	H	E	R	W	P
S	I	E	A	B	Q	D	U	M	T
I	T	S	P	C	A	T	C	H	O
M	E	U	H	S	C	Y	G	E	N
O	B	S	C	I	R	I	C	N	S
N	P	U	Z	G	N	B	O	A	T
I	F	A	L	S	H	G	L	V	E
A	N	Y	T	H	I	N	G	D	N
J	H	O	I	X	E	J	F	M	O
K	L	G	L	K	P	E	T	E	R

SIMON PETER went FISHING all NIGHT but he didn't CATCH ANYTHING. JESUS told him to let down the NETS on the OTHER side of the BOAT. This time they caught LOTS of fish.

Can you fill in the missing bits to see the picture clearly

How to make a fish mobile

You will need:
some string and a shell
6 fish

1 Color the fish and cut them out
2 Thread them on to the string with a knot below each fish so it won't slip
3 Stick a shell to the bottom of the string
4 Make a loop at the top
5 Hang it up and pray it

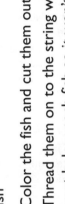

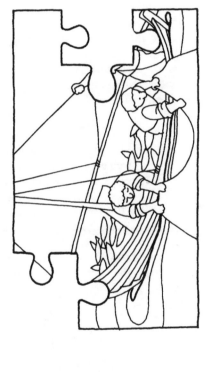

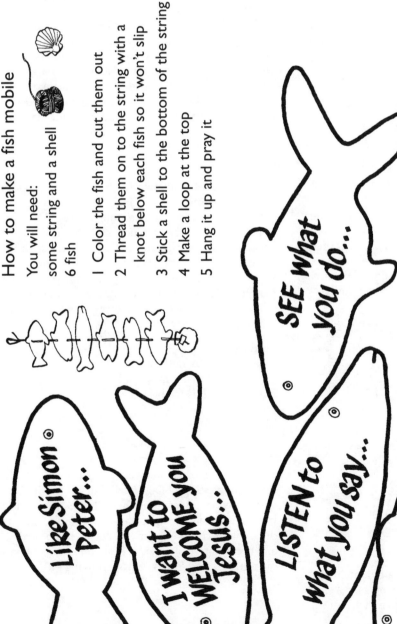

SEE what you do...

Like Simon Peter...

I want to WELCOME you Jesus...

LISTEN to what you say...

GET TO KNOW YOU better...

and FOLLOW YOU all my life.

Sixth Sunday in Ordinary Time

Thought for the day
The challenges and rewards of living by faith.

Readings
Jeremiah 17:5–8
1 Corinthians 15:12, 16–20
Luke 6:17, 20–26

Aim: To think about where we put our trust, and whether this is the best place for it.

Starter
See, I haven't got it! Use a soft ball or beanbag. The children line up across one end of the room and a child at the other end throws the ball into the center of the room before turning away from the other children. The children run to get the ball and whoever has it tries not to show it. The child who threw the ball can ask anyone to turn around and eventually guess who has it.

Teaching
First refer to the starter game. Ask the children who were trying to decide who had the ball if they felt they could trust those who said they didn't have it. (No, they couldn't trust them because the game meant they were hiding the truth.) What or whom can we trust? Today we are going to look at some teaching of Jesus. He was helping people see what they really trusted in. (Use the carpet squares method to tell the story. Pictures needed are shown below.)

Luke tells us that Jesus had been on a mountainside praying all night long before choosing his twelve apostles. They had all agreed to leave their homes and jobs and set out with Jesus. That was a big thing to do, and a lot to give up. Ask the children what might have worried the apostles about their new life and give them some ideas. (Will there be enough to eat? Where will we sleep? Will people think I am stupid? Am I being stupid? Will it be dangerous? Will I be able to do it well enough?)

Jesus brought the apostles to a large level place, and lots of people came to hear what he said. Some of these people were his friends and followers, and some were people who didn't want to follow him because that would mean changing the way they lived and they were comfortable as they were.

First Jesus spoke to the ones who had given up their security to follow him. He told them that the choice they had made—to risk being poor and hungry and sad and insulted, in order to do what was right and good—was a choice that would bring them great rewards of happiness, happiness that would last for ever.

Then he spoke to those who still put all their trust in being rich and having lots of possessions, and doing only what would keep them popular. He told them that we can't get long-term happiness and security from things other people say and make and sell. This kind of richness doesn't last and will leave us poor in the end because it will make us greedy and selfish and never satisfied.

Praying
There is a real challenge to people of all ages in today's teaching, and it is important that we never force children to make decisions or feel they have to believe things they are not ready to. At the same time, it is very important that we give them all the opportunity to voice their love and commitment. Invite the children to join in this prayer having read it to them first. If they don't feel ready to pray it they needn't. Ask them simply to sit quietly so they allow others to pray.

Lord God,
I want to live by faith in you.
I understand that it may not be easy,
but I can see it is the best way to live.
Please show me how.
Thank you. Amen.

Activities
On the activity sheet there are instructions for making a contrasting collage of living rooted in God and rooted in a dry place. The children also explore trust at different levels so they can begin to see the difference between enjoying what God has provided, and becoming so attached to something that it takes over our life and keeps us from moving on.

but . . .

What if one of these stops you

• helping at home
• sharing
• going to church
• being kind

Help me get it right, God

Which of these do you enjoy? Put a ring round them.

Thank you, God, for all these good things.

Jeremiah 17:7-8

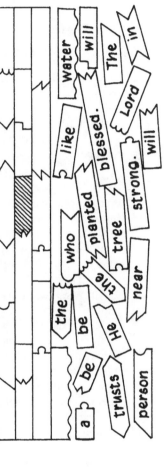

like water will
blessed. The Lord in
who will
planted tree strong.
the near
be He
a be
trusts
person

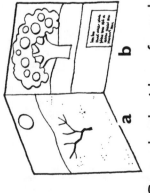

1 Cover both sides of an old card with blue paper
2 For (a) cut out sandpaper and stick on. Stick on a yellow sun and a dead twig.
3 For (b) stick on shiny blue water and green grass. Cut out the brown tree trunk, green leaves and red fruit. Stick them on the background.
4 Cut out this week's prayer and stick it on (b).
5 Stand your collage where you need to be reminded.

This week's prayer

Lord God,
I want to live by faith in you. I understand that it may not be easy, but I can see it is the best way to live.
Please show me how.
Thank you.   Amen.

Seventh Sunday in Ordinary Time

Thought for the day

Jesus teaches us to love our enemies and forgive those who sin against us.

Readings

1 Samuel 26:2, 7–9, 12–13, 22–23
1 Corinthians 15:45–49
Luke 6:27–38

Aim: To explore what it means to love enemies.

Starter

Play any quick softball or beanbag game in two teams, so they experience working against one another. In all these games each side is trying to make it hard for the other. Point out that in the game we are just playing at being on opposite sides or at being enemies.

Teaching

Sit everyone in a circle and pass a card around with the word "enemies" on it. As each person holds the card they say, "An enemy is someone who…" If they don't wish to say anything they just pass the card on. The rule is that only the person holding the card can speak.

Draw all the ideas together, or record them on paper. Then place a card which says "Love your" in front of the other card so they can see Jesus' teaching: Love your enemies. Surely that can't be right? We've just heard all these nasty things about enemies, and here is Jesus telling us to love them. How on earth can we do that? How can we love someone who's always out to get us, and hates us?

Check in the Bible and find that it isn't a mistake; it really says, "love your enemies." Read the passage together.

Ask the children to make their faces full of hate and bitterness. Get them to notice how hard the muscles have to work to do it. It's better and healthier for us not to make a habit of hating and sulking if we're upset, and God knows that. Perhaps they can remember seeing some older people's faces. If we are always thinking life isn't fair, and we hate and resent people, it will show in our faces as we get older. But if we get used to forgiving quickly, and putting the resentment down, that will show in our faces instead. It's right and it's sensible to take Jesus' teaching seriously, even though it is hard to do.

Have the three words of the teaching written on three balloons and learn the teaching by heart by saying it several times, popping one balloon each time.

Praying

Forgive us our trespasses
as we forgive those
who trespass against us. Amen.

Activities

On the activity sheet there are instructions for making a card and envelope to give to someone with whom they need to make up or strengthen a good relationship. The teaching is also reinforced with a code activity.

Notes

R 8

M 12

O 2

Let's be friends again!

Fold

Fold

Color the letters in. Draw your own pictures around the letters. Cut out and fold the sides in.

This week's prayer

Forgive us our trespasses as we forgive those who trespass against us.

Amen.

E 14 4 9 11

U 7

Keep it to give to someone you want to make up with and forgive.

Y 5

S 15

V 3

L 1

I 13

Decorate the net. Fold it into an envelope and stick the edges. Put in the card and stick the envelope down.

N 10

		1	2	3	4
		5	6	7	8

	9	10	11	12	13	14	15

Eighth Sunday in Ordinary Time

Thought for the day

What we think is important flows out in the way we speak.

Readings

Sirach 27:4–7
1 Corinthians 15:54–58
Luke 6:39–45

Aim: To know Jesus' teaching about hypocrisy.

Starter

Play one of those card games when you pretend about which card you have put down. If you are challenged and found to have cheated, then you have to take back all the cards on the table.

Teaching

Point out how cheating can be fun in a game like that, but real cheating in life is wrong and very bad for us. Jesus could see that whenever people tried to cheat themselves or God, they ended up in a bad way, and today we are going to hear some of the funny cartoons Jesus used to help us understand the importance of being honest with ourselves and honest with God.

Use these drawings below to make large cartoon pictures with captions, and display them in turn, discussing them with the children and helping them understand how silly it is for one blindfolded person to offer to guide another, or for someone blinded by a great plank in his eye offer to take a tiny splinter out of someone else's eye.

How are we sometimes like these silly people? It's always when we aren't being honest with ourselves. We pretend to ourselves that we don't have any faults ourselves, but we keep moaning about everyone else's faults. And that, says Jesus, is cheating, or something called *hypocrisy*. To have a good relationship with God, we need to stop all that and get real with ourselves. Then God can work in us to help us become good trees which keep producing good fruit.

Praying

Father God, help me
to be more honest with you
and with myself.
I know there isn't any point
in trying to pretend with you
because you know my deepest thoughts
and I can hide nothing from you.

Activities

On the activity sheet there are some short scripts for the children to try which help them explore what hypocrisy is, and how it goes against all God's love and truth and faithfulness.

Notes

THE H-FILES

Katie   Hey, stop copying my work, Paul.

Paul   Well, you just down-loaded it from the internet! What's that if it isn't copying?

Katie   That's different – and don't <u>tell</u> everyone.

Paul   Oh, Katie!

All: Don't be such a hypocrite [hip - o - crit]!

THE H-FILES

Jay $300.00 altogether for my birthday. Hee hee, I'm rich. (EMMA COMES IN)

Emma   Can you give some money to help children in need? (SHE RATTLES BOX)

Jay   No, sorry – I haven't got enough money.

All: Don't be such a hypocrite [hip - o - crit]!

THE H-FILES

Tom   Shall I invite Ben?

Daisy   No – he hasn't got much money, so he won't give us a big present.

Tom   What about Pat?

Daisy   Yes, be really nice to Pat – she's rich.

All: Don't be such a hypocrite [hip - o - crit]!

This word is a kind of cheating, like when you pretend to be kind but really you are not being kind at all . . . but are horrible to everyone . . . this is something that Jesus hated to see because he wants us to try and be honest with God or when you go to church and pray

To pray this week

Father God, help me to be more honest with you and with myself. I know there isn't any point in trying to pretend with you because you know my deepest thoughts and I can hide nothing from you.

Ninth Sunday in Ordinary Time

Thought for the day

The good news we have been given is not just for us, but to pass on to the rest of the world.

Readings

1 Kings 8:41–43
Galatians 1:1–2, 6–10
Luke 7:1–10

Aim: To understand the meaning of Jewish, Gentile and Christian, and to look at who can be what.

Starter

Have an alphabetical list of all the different last names of the children, so that those in the same family or sharing the same last name will be listed together. Talk briefly about where some of these names come from originally. Then play some music with everyone dancing and moving around until you call out a name, or a letter. Only the members of these families can keep on moving; the others must freeze until you call another name out.

Teaching

Explain that we are members of our family because we were born or adopted into it, and that when we read about the Jewish people in the Bible, it means people who were born as members of the Jewish race which could be traced back to Abraham. No one else could be Jewish, and God chose the Jewish people to work through. Through them all the other nations would eventually be brought to know God's saving love. Jesus was born into a Jewish family, so he was Jewish. Anyone who isn't Jewish by birth is called a Gentile, and as we often hear about Gentiles in the Bible as well, it's a good idea to know about them.

Have two hoops labeled "Jewish" and "Gentile" and some names written on small cards. As a group, decide which names should go in which hoop. (Suggestions for names: Abraham, Goliath, Joseph, Moses, Pharaoh, Jesus, Mary, Peter, Paul, St. Francis and the names of some of the children.)

Now take the hoops and names away and replace them with one hoop labeled "Christian—a follower of Christ." Scatter around the hoop cards with these categories written on them: women, men, boys, girls; people with black skin, people with pink skin; people who go to (N.   ) school, people who support a rival sports team; Jewish people, Gentile people, old people, rich people, poor peo-

ple. Ask them to put in the hoop those they think can be Christians and leave outside those who can't. Draw them to the realization that everybody can be a follower of Jesus Christ, and the good news of God's love is for everybody everywhere to enjoy.

Praying

Dear Jesus,
we pray for those
who have not heard of you
and do not know you.
Give us the opportunity
to share the good news
with someone today. Amen.

Activities

The activity sheet encourages them to look at how they can spread the good news, and gives examples of people who have been called to tell others the gospel even though it put them in danger.

Notes

Draw or write what you would want people to know about God.

Jackie Pullinger
DRUGS
city

Jackie Pullinger lived and worked with the drug addicts in Hong Kong. She wanted them to know the power of Jesus in their lives. As they started to trust her, many came to know God, and it changed their lives.

Brother Andrew
SMUGGLER
of Bibles

Brother Andrew found out that people in parts of Russia and China were not allowed to have Bibles for sale. So he smuggled Bibles across the borders and made sure people could read the good news. He was often in great danger.

Father Damien
LEPROSY
Island

Father Damien chose to live on an island where lepers had to live, so that he could teach them about God's love, and help them. He did get leprosy himself through working with the disease.

How could you spread the Good News

using these

To pray this week

Dear Jesus,
we pray for those who have not heard of you and do not know you. Give us the opportunity to share the good news with someone today.
Amen.

Tenth Sunday in Ordinary Time

Thought for the day

Our God is full of compassion; he hears our crying and it is his nature to rescue us.

Readings

1 Kings 17:17–24
Galatians 1:11–19
Luke 7:11–17

Aim: To know that God is tenderly interested in us in the heartbreak as well as the happy times.

Starter

Using a long bamboo cane balanced across two people's hands, play "higher and higher," with the children taking turns to jump over the ever-increasing height. (Make sure the cane will fall as soon as it's touched, so that no one gets hurt.)

Teaching

In that high-jump exercise we were finding our limits. We discovered how high we could jump and what was just too much for us at the moment until we grow taller. Sometimes life can feel a bit like the high jump, when we are expected to do harder and harder things, and cope with bigger and bigger hurts, until we feel we can't cope with much more.

Today we have two amazing examples of how much God loves and cares for us in the sad times of our lives, as well as when everything is going well. One event is from the Old Testament, long before Jesus had been born, and the other is from the New Testament, when Jesus was walking about on earth. Introduce two women, who can be leaders or volunteers brought in specially. They are dressed in costume, or at least with cloths over their heads. You are going to interview them both.

First introduce the widow of Zarephath, and interview her so that the story of her great sadness and anger are brought out because of her son's illness and death, as well as the amazing way God showed his love through Elijah. (Make sure you are both very familiar with the whole story as told in 1 Kings 17, and talk together in a relaxed and natural way.)

Then turn to the other woman, also a widow, and interview her in the same way, bringing out her great sorrow and fears for the future, and the love shown to her through the way Jesus speaks to her and to her son. Then ask both women what the experience has taught them about God. The widow of Zarephath can say how it has helped her to know that this God (whom she didn't know before) seems to be completely faithful and loving. The widow of Nain can say how it has helped her to know that God must be interested in ordinary people and their troubles, and want to help them. He must be even more powerful than death.

Thank the two visitors and invite them to stay for the rest of Explorers this morning.

Praying

Lord, whenever we pray,
you are listening.
Whenever we are crying,
you share in our sadness,
and whenever we are happy,
you share in our joy.
Your love always surrounds us.
Amen.

Activities

On a world map find out where Zarephath is. (It's midway between Tyre and Sidon, on the Mediterranean coast.) The activity sheet encourages them to sympathize with both widows, and this can lead on to praying for those in the news at the moment who must be very sad.

Notes

QUIZ

A Which town was Jesus visiting?

B Was the woman married, widowed or divorced?

C Was it a son or a daughter who had died?

D Why did Jesus stop at the coffin?

E What did Jesus say to the dead person?

F What did the crowds say?

Look up the answers in Luke 7:11–17

To pray this week

Lord, whenever we pray, you are listening.
Whenever we are crying, you share in our sadness,
and whenever we are happy you share in our joy.
Your love always surrounds us. Amen.

full of joy

impressed

hopeful

sorry for yourself

sad

angry

sorry for your son

frightened

I Kings 17:17-24

How would you feel if you were the boy's mom?

Can you put in Zarepath?

OUR GOD IS FULL OF

AND

Mediterranean Sea

Beirut

Sidon

Tyre

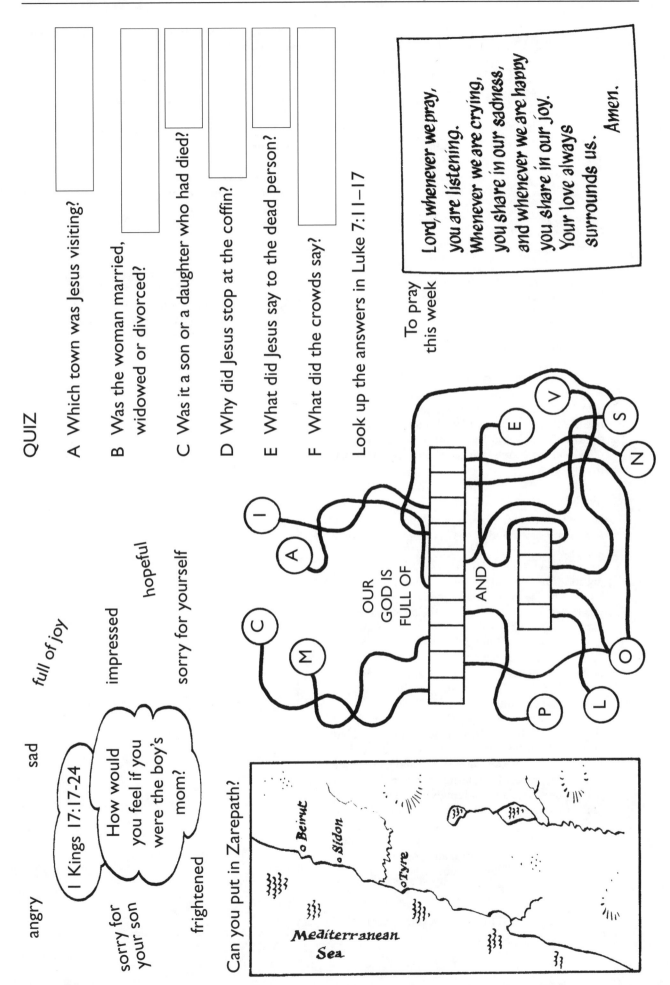

Eleventh Sunday in Ordinary Time

Thought for the day

God has the authority and the desire to forgive our sins completely and set us free from guilt.

Readings

2 Samuel 12:7–10, 13
Galatians 2:16, 19–21
Luke 7:36—8:3

Aim: To know that God can help us face up to our sin as well as forgive and set us free.

Starter

Sit in a circle. Each person in turn says three things about someone in the circle (only positives allowed), and everyone guesses who it is. Each person can only be described once, which means that everyone gets a turn to be described. Or play "Stuck in the mud," which is a kind of "tag." When caught, you stand with arms and legs apart, stuck in the mud, unless someone crawls through your legs to set you free again.

Teaching

Set up the circle as if you are all guests at a meal, with a tablecloth, and plates of things to eat, which are handed around as you tell the children about a meal Jesus was invited to at a grand house belonging to a Pharisee called Simon. Simon thought of himself as a good person, something of an expert where God was concerned. At the meal something happened which Jesus used to help Simon see himself as not very loving or forgiving.

As you explain about the woman coming in, bring out some perfumed oil and rub a little in the palms of your hands so that the children can smell the fragrance as you speak.

Continue relating how Simon was indignant about this and thought Jesus should know what kind of bad woman this was, if he really was a prophet. When you tell the story Jesus told Simon, invite the children to answer the question before telling them what Simon (rather grudgingly) answered. Then finish by telling how Jesus used this story to help Simon understand himself better and give him the opportunity to put things right with God. God never makes us do things against our will, but he does all he can to help us choose what is right.

Praying

Talk about our need to recognize and admit to God the times when we let him down by our unloving, selfish behavior, knowing that he is able to forgive us.

Lord God,
thank you for helping me do good today,
when I ...
I am sorry that I let you down
and hurt others
when I ...
Please forgive me
and help me put it right.
Thank you, Lord God,
for forgiving me!

Activities

On the activity sheet there are instructions for making a "soul mirror"; each child will need either a small hand mirror or shiny mirror paper. There is also an activity to reinforce the teaching and encourage discussion about the gospel.

Notes

How to make a mirror to check your behavior in

What you do

1 Cut the paper to the size of the mirror
2 Draw a cross on it and cut it out
3 Write on the surrounding paper: 'Look at my love for you. How was your love today?'

Use your 'soul mirror' at night and let God forgive you.

You will need

a small mirror

blutack

scissors

paper

To pray during the week

Lord God,
Thank you for helping me do good today when I . . . .
I am sorry that I let you down and hurt others when I . . . .
Please forgive me, and help me put it right.
Thank you, Lord God, for forgiving me!

Who did what?

Luke 7:36—8:3

Jesus

This person thought he was a good person who God was proud of

This person loved God a lot because she knew she had been forgiven for a lot

This character in the story was the most grateful

The woman who washed Jesus' feet with her tears

This person told a story to reflect the truth into Simon's eyes

Simon

Twelfth Sunday in Ordinary Time

Thought for the day
Following Christ means daily taking up our cross.

Readings
Zechariah 12:10–11; 13:1
Galatians 3:26–29
Luke 9:18–24

Aim: To help them understand how brokenness and dying are necessary for new life.

Starter
Unpack a fresh wad of modeling clay and break it up, sharing it among everyone so they can make something with it. Display the models and remind everyone how necessary it was to break the beautifully packaged modeling clay in order to make all these creative new things with it.

Teaching
Read to the children the story of the crucifixion from a children's Bible version (such as *The Road to the Cross* from the Palm Tree series, or an excerpt from *Donkey's Glory* by Nan Goodall) or show one of the children's video versions. (Think carefully about what you use, as it is important that you choose something suitable for your particular group.)

Explain how Jesus knew that all this was bound to happen to him, and he didn't try to escape from it, even though it scared him. He did it because he knew it was the only way to save us—through going on and on loving and forgiving right through everything.

All the violence and pain directed toward Jesus is difficult for them to cope with, and it may help them to see how beans have to break apart to allow new growth. Show them a jar with germinated beans between damp blotting paper and the glass, so that they can see how the bean needs to be broken before new life can come from it.

Jesus said that anyone wanting to be his follower would have to be prepared to give themselves up like this. Draw a capital I on a large sheet. When we cross out selfishness (cross out the capital I) what shape does it make? The shape of Jesus' cross.

Praying
Jesus, your unselfish loving
led you to the pain of the cross.
Thank you for loving us that much.
Help us to follow you
in unselfish loving
even if it hurts. Amen.

Activities
On the activity sheet there are instructions for planting their own beans in jars (they will each need a jar, damp blotting paper or cotton wadding, and beans). There is also a picture of the crucifixion for them to color and mount the prayer on.

Notes

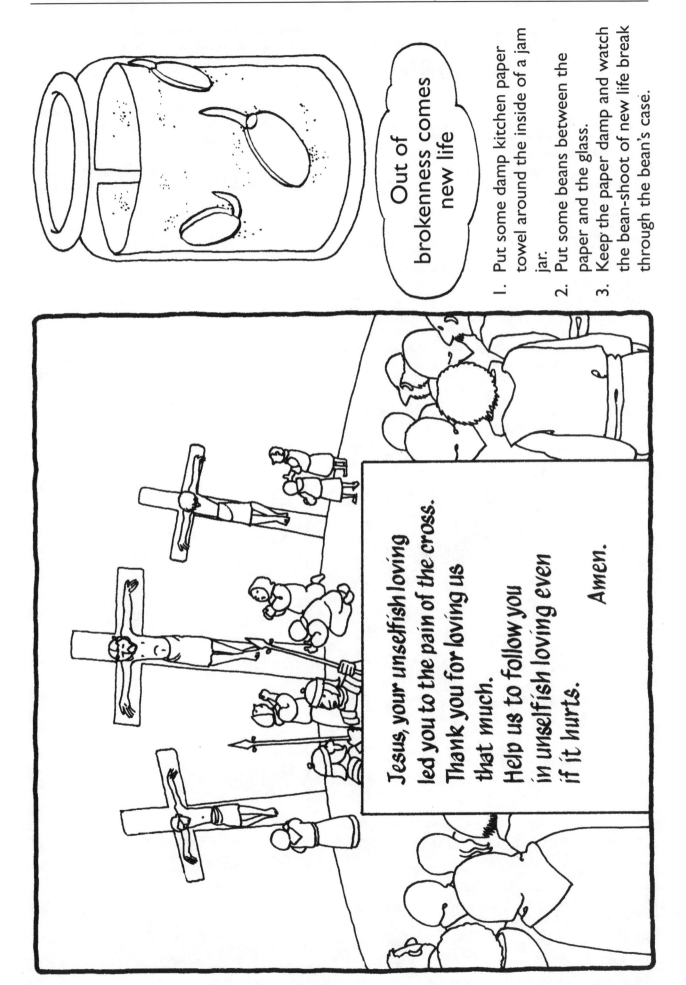

Out of brokenness comes new life

1. Put some damp kitchen paper towel around the inside of a jam jar.
2. Put some beans between the paper and the glass.
3. Keep the paper damp and watch the bean-shoot of new life break through the bean's case.

Jesus, your unselfish loving led you to the pain of the cross. Thank you for loving us that much. Help us to follow you in unselfish loving even if it hurts.

Amen.

Thirteenth Sunday in Ordinary Time

Thought for the day
When we are called to follow Jesus, that means total commitment, with no half-measures.

Readings
1 Kings 19:16, 19–21
Galatians 5:1, 13–18
Luke 9:51–62

Aim: To get to know the story of Elisha responding to Elijah's call.

Starter
What's my line? Taking turns the children mime a job, and everyone has to guess what it is. The one who guesses correctly does the next mime, or you can go around the group circle.

Teaching
Prepare the different pictures for the story on paper. Suggestions are given below.

Then tell the story using carpet squares on the floor and move the pictures around as you talk.

Praying
Lord God, here I am,
ready to do
whatever you need me to.

And, Lord, prepare me now
for what you would like me to do
in the future. Amen.

Activities
The activity sheet explores the nature of vocation, with quotations from people in varied ministries. Talk through with the children the ministry they have in places no one but they can reach, such as in their families and friendships, on their playground and at their clubs. Jesus likes to use us where we are.

Notes

Draw in Elisha with his 12 yoke of oxen

Knock knock.
Who's there?
Ivor.
Ivor who?
Ivor message for you, if only you'd listen!

Knock knock.
Who's there?
You.
You who?
That's *my* line!

To pray this week

Lord God, here I am, ready to do whatever you need me to.

What did Elijah do with his cloak?

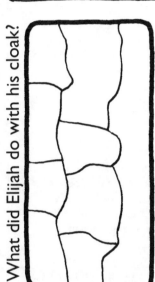

I Kings 19:19-21

near   and

over   his   threw

cloak

came   Elijah   Elisha

Being called by God to a particular job is sometimes known as having a

Here are some people talking about what they were called to do.

When I was 6 years old I knew I wanted to be a priest, and felt God had called me. I love helping people get to know God, though it can be hard work.

I was already an athlete and when I became a Christian God called me to use my work in sports to bring people to Christ. It makes life twice as exciting!

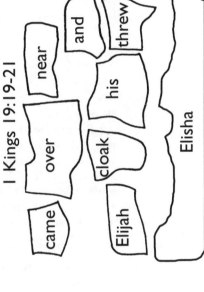

I felt God was calling me to serve him by teaching the children at church. They teach me as much as I teach them!

God gave us the idea of this rock band, and now we sing and play to young people and it's exciting to lead them to God through our music

Fourteenth Sunday in Ordinary Time

Thought for the day
In Christ we become a new creation.

Readings
Isaiah 66:10–14
Galatians 6:14–18
Luke 10:1–12, 17–20

Aim: To hear about the seventy-two being sent out by Jesus.

Starter
Send people out in pairs with matchboxes, on a mission to collect six different things which fit in their box. Show one another the results when everyone gets back. You can make this a timed activity if your schedule is tight.

Teaching
First fill in the background to this mission. Jesus began by doing the teaching and healing all over the local area, training his followers or disciples as he went. Jesus realizes that there are huge numbers of people all ready to hear the good news, but only a few people to teach them. He talks about it as being like a huge harvest of people, ripe to gather in, but with very few workers to do it. So now he spreads the net wider, by sending out seventy-two of his trained followers. As this is quite a large number to visualize, have seventy-two paper people cut out and spread them all over the floor in the middle of the circle. Let a few children put them into pairs because Jesus sent these people out in pairs. They can discuss the advantages of this.

Jesus gathered this crowd of people together and gave them their instructions. Have these written out on a large sheet of paper or length of wallpaper:

1. Be careful.
2. Travel light.
3. Don't waste time chatting on the way.
4. "Peace to this house!"
5. Eat what you are given.
6. Heal the sick in body and mind.
7. Tell them the kingdom of God is very close to them.

Use the instruction list on the activity sheet with its picture symbols as you tell the children what happened, and how excited they were when they got back because of the many ways God had blessed their work.

Praying
Lord, so many people
have no idea how happy they could be
with you at the center of their life.
Please send us lots more workers
into this harvest,
to let the people know about you
and bring them safely into your kingdom.

Activities
Using the cut-out people and a large sheet of paper, make a collage picture of this mission, sticking on the children's drawings of roads, villages, trees and the people hearing the good news everywhere, and being healed. The activity sheet has a copy of the list of instructions given to the seventy-two.

Notes

Jesus told the disciples

'The – – – – – – – is rich but the laborers are – – –'.

To pray this week

Lord, so many people have no idea of how happy they could be with you at the centre of their life. Please send us lots more workers into this harvest, to let the people know about you and bring them safely into your kingdom.   Amen.

MATH

How many?

... instructions? ☐

... workers sent out? ☐

... pairs of workers? ☐

... feet? ☐

TOTAL LOTS!

(And that's how many more workers are needed LOTS!)

Who do you know, who is working on God's harvest? Write their names here. Pray for them.

INSTRUCTIONS

1 Be careful

2 Travel light

3 Don't waste time chatting on the way

4 'Peace to this house!'

5 Eat what you are given

6 Heal the sick in body and mind

7 Tell them the kingdom of God is very close to them

How would you feel about living like this?

Fifteenth Sunday in Ordinary Time

Thought for the day

Straighten your lives out and live by God's standards of love.

Readings

Deuteronomy 30:10–14
Colossians 1:15–20
Luke 10:25–37

Aim: To know the story and context of "The Good Samaritan."

Starter

Sit in a circle and first ask everyone to find out the favorite color or food of the person on their left. Now go around the circle with each person introducing their neighbor—"This is Charlie and his favorite color is dark metallic green."

Teaching

Read verse 25 from the gospel, and ask the children what they think Jesus might have said. Explain that he didn't actually give the expert an answer, but another question. (Read verse 26.) Remind the children of what it does say in the Law as the two "life rules"—have it written up so you can all read it out together: "Love the Lord your God with all your heart and with all your soul and with all your mind, and love your neighbor as yourself."

Now ask a child to read Jesus' reply in verse 28. Explain that the expert didn't feel it should be as simple as that ("experts" often like things to be very complicated) and, also, the experts didn't much like the way Jesus was mixing with all the wrong sort of people.

So Jesus told them a story to teach them that loving our neighbor is more than being nice to those we happen to like.

Tell the story, drawing it as you go on a blackboard with colored chalks. The drawings don't need to be grand, but will help the children focus, and the simpler the drawings are, the more their imaginations can work.

At the end of the story, read the question Jesus asked (verse 36). The expert had to admit that it was the unliked foreigner who had actually been living by God's law of loving care.

Praying

Lord God,
help me to notice
when other people need my help,
and remind me to do
what I can to help them. Amen.

Activities

On the activity sheet there are pictures of the story to which they add various things, and also some space to write in the names of their own neighbors, so they can pray for them. They can try measuring up their own lives against the summary of the Law, so that they begin to understand that loving sometimes involves doing things we may not want to do at all.

Notes

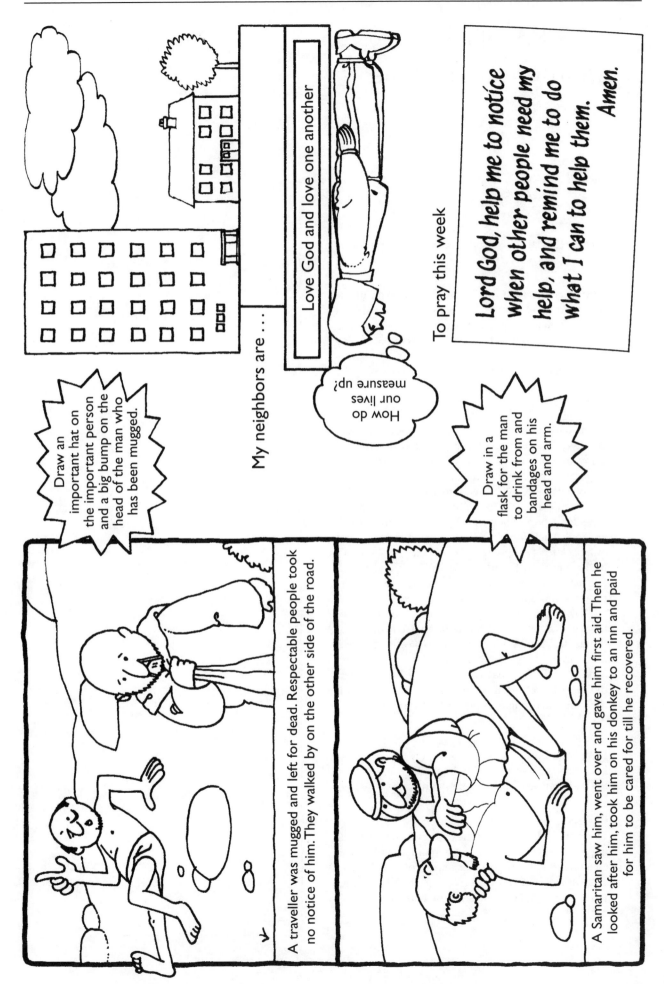

Sixteenth Sunday in Ordinary Time

Thought for the day
Attentive listening is all part of serving.

Readings
Genesis 18:1–10
Colossians 1:24–28
Luke 10:38–42

Aim: To look at the importance of listening to God.

Starter
Sit in a circle, with one blindfolded person in the center. Another person creeps round the outside of the circle with a jangling set of keys. The blindfolded person points to where the person is. If they are right they take the keys and a new person is blindfolded.

Teaching
Begin with a sketch to express the busy nature of our lives. It will need to be prepared beforehand using one or two of the children. An alarm clock rings and the children dash in with pajamas and teddy bears. They pretend to eat their breakfast really quickly, and grab their books and pencilcases for school. They dash back in for lunchboxes, and out, back for gym clothes or equivalent, and out, back for swimming gear, and out, back for violin or equivalent, and out, back to sit and watch television and eat something, and out, in wearing pajamas and teddy bears again, and out.

Talk about what the children do on each day of the week and how nice it is to be able to do all these things, but how important it is to stop and spend quiet times every day with God. Have the children acting out the Martha and Mary story, bringing out the need to get the listening times right so that all the practical doing falls properly into place.

Praying
Here I am, Lord.
I have come to spend some time with you,
to sit at your feet and be quiet with you.

Activities
There are instructions on the activity sheet for making a prayer corner for their bedroom, to be used as a reminder for daily prayer and a focus for them. There is also a prayer pattern using a hand drawing, which can be cut out and stuck on to the prayer corner.

Notes

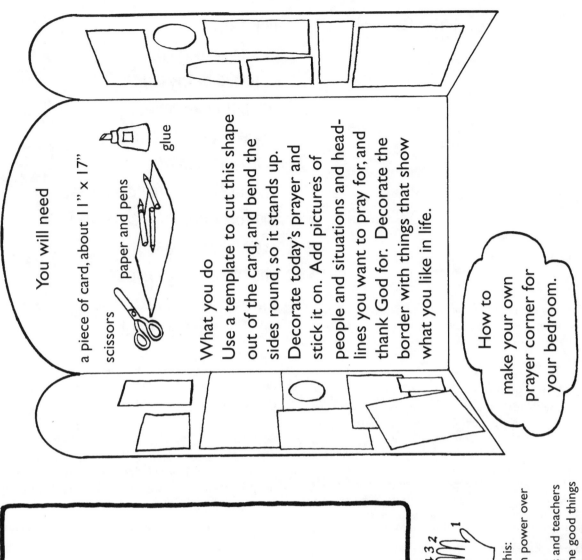

How to make your own prayer corner for your bedroom.

You will need

a piece of card, about 11" x 17"

scissors

paper and pens

glue

What you do
Use a template to cut this shape out of the card, and bend the sides round, so it stands up. Decorate today's prayer and stick it on. Add pictures of people and situations and headlines you want to pray for, and thank God for. Decorate the border with things that show what you like in life.

Draw around your hand and cut it

Label each finger like this:
1 Pray for people with power over others
2 Pray for our leaders and teachers
3 Thank God for all the good things
4 Pray for family and friends
5 Pray for yourself and your needs

Here I am, Lord. I have come to spend some time with you, to sit at your feet and be quiet with you.

Seventeenth Sunday in Ordinary Time

Thought for the day
Keep asking for God's Spirit and he will keep pouring out his blessing on you.

Readings
Genesis 18:20–32
Colossians 2:12–24
Luke 11:1–13

Aim: To look at the meaning of the Lord's prayer.

Starter
Play a game of hide and seek, or sardines, or look for a hidden object, with clues of "hotter" or "colder" only being given if they are asked for.

Teaching
Jesus often used to go off on his own to talk things over with his Father in heaven and listen to his Father's advice. Sometimes they would just be quiet in one another's company. These times helped Jesus have the wisdom and energy he needed to do his work, as we mentioned last week.

His followers could see how useful those times were to Jesus, and they wanted to do it themselves but they didn't know how to. So they asked Jesus to teach them all how to pray. And this is what Jesus suggested they do.

1. Remember that God is your Father in heaven, and that he is holy.

2. Ask for the kingdom of God to come, and God's will to be done.

3. Ask for enough to eat and for your needs for the day.

4. Ask God to forgive your sins, just as you have forgiven people who have upset you.

5. Ask God to lead you safely through temptation and out of evil.

Have them written up on separate cards, and answer any questions about each one as you go along. Jumble them up and invite a couple of children to put them in the right order again. Then have someone reading each one out, and a pause for everyone to do what the card says. Introducing them to the meaning like this, before the traditional words, will prevent understanding being blocked by familiar but undigested words.

Now see if any of them know the traditional form of this teaching, known as the Lord's Prayer. Teach them these actions to do as they say it, to make sure they are praying, and not just reciting some instructions.

Our Father,
who art in heaven,
hallowed be thy name;
thy kingdom come;
thy will be done on earth
as it is in heaven. (LOOK UP)
(LOOK DOWN)
Give us this day our daily bread; (CUP HANDS)
and forgive us our trespasses
as we forgive those
who trespass against us;
and lead us not into temptation,
but deliver us from evil.
Amen.

Praying
Use the Lord's Prayer with actions.

Activities
The instructions are written on the activity sheet so that they can be colored, decorated and stuck on to the prayer corner made last week. There is also an activity looking at giving and gifts.

Notes

What on earth is he wanting? (Luke 11:1–13)

To pray this week

Our Father, who art in heaven,
hallowed be thy name;
thy kingdom come;
thy will be done on earth
as it is in heaven.
Give us this day our daily bread;
and forgive us our trespasses,
as we forgive those who trespass against us;
and lead us not into temptation,
but deliver us from evil.
     Amen.

How often should I pray to God?

When I feel like it

Every day

Once a month

YES!

Can you 'seek' the answer?

Knock knock!
Who's there?
Ivan.
Ivan who?
Ivan unexpected guest and we need some bread!

Teach us to pray

1 Remember that God is your Father in heaven, and that he is holy.

2 Ask for the kingdom of God to come, and God's will to be done.

3 Ask for enough to eat and for your needs for the day.

4 Ask God to forgive your sins, just as you have forgiven people who have upset you.

5 Ask God to lead you safely through temptation and out of evil.

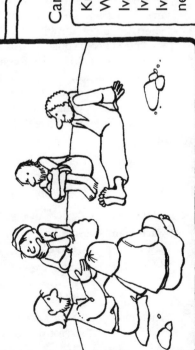

Eighteenth Sunday in Ordinary Time

Thought for the day

True richness is not material wealth; true security is not a financial matter.

Readings

Sirach 1:2; 2:21–23
Colossians 3:1–5, 9–11
Luke 12:13–21

Aim: To look at real lasting wealth.

Starter

My aunt went to Paris. Sit in a circle. The first person says, "My aunt went to Paris and she bought a …" They name something and mime it at the same time. The next person has to say this item followed by their own, and so on.

Teaching

Have a tape recording of excerpts from several current TV advertisements, and they can guess what item is being advertised. Point out that the fact we know these means that the advertisements are working. Although this is good for the company who makes the chocolate or car, it can encourage us to be greedy, and discontented.

Show the children a timeline with "Now" at the left end, an ongoing arrow at the right end and a point marked "Death" about a third of the way along the line. Remind the children that our new life in Christ doesn't stop at death, but goes on for ever in heaven. The bit on earth here is only quite a short section of our whole life.

Lots of people put their trust in money and things, rather than in God. They forget that these can only last up to death, at the very most. Spiritual treasure, however, is long-lasting, forever.

Tell the story of the rich fool, using the script below.

Music from Beethoven's *Pastoral Symphony* fades in.

Narrator	There was once a rich man who had a very good harvest.
	(Sound of running)
Slave	Master! Master!
Rich man	*(Snoring; wakes up)* Oh! Yes—what is it, slave?
Slave	Master, we've filled all the barns with the crops but there's still lots more left to store.
Rich man	*(Laughs)* Well, well! Such a good harvest that there's no room to store

my crops, eh? Now what can I do about that, I wonder.

Slave	Perhaps you could give some away?
Rich man	What! Good heavens, no! I know what I'll do. Slave—start pulling the barns down.
Slave	Pull them down, Master? B…b…but we've only just filled them up.
Rich man	Then empty them, you fool! We're going to build *enormous* barns—enough to hold all my grain.
Slave	Very well, Master; your wish is my command. *(Runs off. His voice is heard in the distance)* Come on, lads, get busy. All the grain is to be moved.
Other slaves	*(Groaning)* Oh no! What on earth for? After all that work!
	(Sounds of workers pouring grain fades into music. Music fades into building sounds.)
Slave driver	Come on there, stop wasting time.
	(Sound of whip)
Rich man	Ah, good, the new barns are splendid! Keep up the good work. *(Music fades in)* Now I've got so much grain I can enjoy myself for years to come. I think I'll start with a feast. No more worries for me! *(Sounds of eating and drinking)*
	(Cymbal, or saucepan lids)
God	Fool! Fool! *(Cymbal)*
Rich man	*(Flustered)* Eh? Oh, my goodness, who said that?
	(Cymbal)
God	I, God, tell you that you are a fool! This very night you are going to die. What use will your hoard of grain be to you then? *(Cymbal)* What use will your hoard of grain be to you then?
	(Music fades in to finish)
Narrator	So the man saw that getting rich did not make him safe and secure.

Praying

Thank you, Father,
for showing us a new way to live,
trusting in your love
and building treasure in heaven.

Activities

On the activity sheet there is an activity to help them weigh the better bargain: being rich or being loved—being happy because you've just bought a CD or being happy because you know God loves you? Try making the script into a radio play, with sound effects. It could then be used for a parish performance, or study day.

Draw a cartoon strip story called 'The foolish lottery winner'

Winning	Spending	?

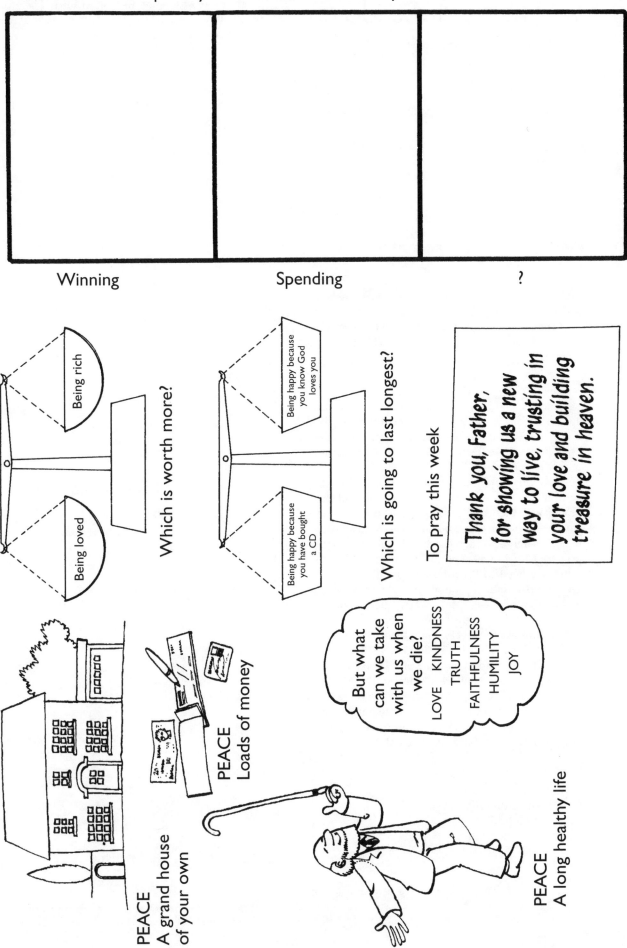

Which is worth more?

Being rich

Being loved

Which is going to last longest?

Being happy because you know God loves you

Being happy because you have bought a CD

To pray this week

Thank you, Father, for showing us a new way to live, trusting in your love and building treasure in heaven.

But what can we take with us when we die?

LOVE   KINDNESS
TRUTH
FAITHFULNESS
HUMILITY
JOY

PEACE
A grand house of your own

PEACE
Loads of money

PEACE
A long healthy life

Nineteenth Sunday in Ordinary Time

firefighters getting ready to rush to a fire. The quiz linked to it can be used to start discussion about our spiritual readiness. There is a cartoon to draw to reinforce the teaching, and an activity which requires Bibles so they can look up the Luke references.

Thought for the day
Have faith in God, and get yourself ready to meet him.

Readings
Wisdom 18:6–9
Hebrews 11:1–2, 8–19
Luke 12:32–48

Aim: To know the importance of keeping ready.

Starter
"What's the time, Mr. Wolf?" or a similar "creeping-up" kind of game. Talk about the way you had to keep alert because you didn't know exactly when you were going to have to run, or when Mr. Wolf would turn around.

Teaching
Remind the children that after Jesus died and rose again he went to live in heaven. (Let them tell you, if they know.) But one day he will come back, and he hopes that we'll still be watchful and ready for him when he comes.

How do people keep themselves prepared for helping at accidents? They learn first aid and they practice so they don't forget. How do we make sure we're prepared for a bike race? We learn how to cycle safely and then practice. What about being prepared for Jesus—how can we do that? It's the same; we need to learn how to live his way and then keep practicing. Point out that they are all learning week by week when they come to Explorers, and when they read the Bible. They practice all through the week, doing their praying, and choosing how to behave. Sometimes we get it wrong, but the important thing is to keep trying.

Get some of the children to act out the parables of the master finding the faithful servants and waiting on them for a change, and the burglars not being able to rob the house because the owner is being very tiresome and keeping watch.

Praying
Lord Jesus,
I want you to find me
watching faithfully
when you come again.

Activities
On the activity sheet there is a picture to color of

Notes

Luke 12:32-34

Don't ———, little ——— .

Your F——— wants to g——— you the k——— .

S—l the things you h——— .

G——— to the ——— .

Get yourselves p——— that don't w——— out.

Get the tr——— in h——— that never runs out.

Your h——t will be where your t——— is.

To pray this week

Lord Jesus,
I want you to find me
watching faithfully
when you come again.
Amen.

This is a burglar being caught by the owner of the house

Ready and waiting!

Who is getting ready here?

nurses	
firefighters	
soldiers	

Where are they off to?

a shipwreck	
a party	
a fire	

How do they know what to do?

they're in training	
they don't know	
they watched Fireman Sam	

Twentieth Sunday in Ordinary Time

Thought for the day

When we fix our eyes on Jesus our lives will reflect his nature.

Readings

Jeremiah 38:4–6, 8–10
Hebrews 12:1–4
Luke 12:49–53

Aim: To learn about fixing our eyes on Jesus and running the race unhindered.

Starter

Loads of fun. This team game involves the first team member running up to a point, collecting a heavy bag and lugging it back to the team. The second team member lugs it back, dumps it and runs back. The next person does the same, and so on. The team with most luggage journeys logged in the time allocated wins.

Teaching

Point out how much everyone was slowed down by the weight of the luggage, and also how much easier it is to run to the right place if we look where we're going.

Bring out an envelope (stamped and addressed) and explain how some of the early Christian leaders wrote letters to keep in touch with the churches. The Bible has collected some of these old letters, written nearly two thousand years ago, so that we can still read them today. So this letter (not the actual envelope, though!) has been around a very long time. We're not even sure who wrote it, but it's got such useful hints in it that it's well worth reading.

Take out the letter, and read the first introductory section to Hebrews, followed by the *International Children's Bible* (New Century) version of today's reading. Draw attention to how it fits in with what we found in our game, about running lightly and carefully and focusing on Jesus.

Talk about people who can't enjoy what they've got because they're always wishing they had something better or different, and it turns them into unhappy moaners. God wants them to be free of the "wanting" so they can enjoy life, no matter what they have or haven't got.

Talk about people who want to boss their friends around all the time, and end up without friends or with people scared of them. Their bossiness and bullying is like a heavy bag they're carrying, and it keeps them from really enjoying life. God wants

them to put it down so they can play with other children and be happy.

If we are carrying any habits like moaning or bossiness, or keeping an enemy or upsetting someone all the time, the writer of this letter from the Roman world is saying, "Why don't you put that down today, and focus your eyes on Jesus, so you can live free and happy?"

Praying

Lord Jesus,
I'm going to run the race
with my eyes
focused on you.
And if I get cluttered
with silly or bad habits,
please remind me
to put them down
so I can run free.

Activities

On the activity sheet there are instructions for making a race game. It requires two fridge magnets for each child.

Notes

GO FOR IT!

To pray this week

Lord Jesus,
I'm going to run the race with my eyes fixed on you. And if I get cluttered with silly or bad habits, please remind me to put them down so I can run free.
Amen.

How to make a moving runner!
You will need thin card, pens and scissors, 2 pieces of fridge magnet

What you do
1 Color and cut out the pieces as shown.
2 Fix on the magnets with glue, with the arrow in front of the race track and the runner behind it.
3 Fix the ends of the race track to a door or wall with blutack
4 As you read the words on the track, move the arrow towards the cross, and the runner will come as well!

Complete the words. Color the cross. Stick on thin card, and cut out

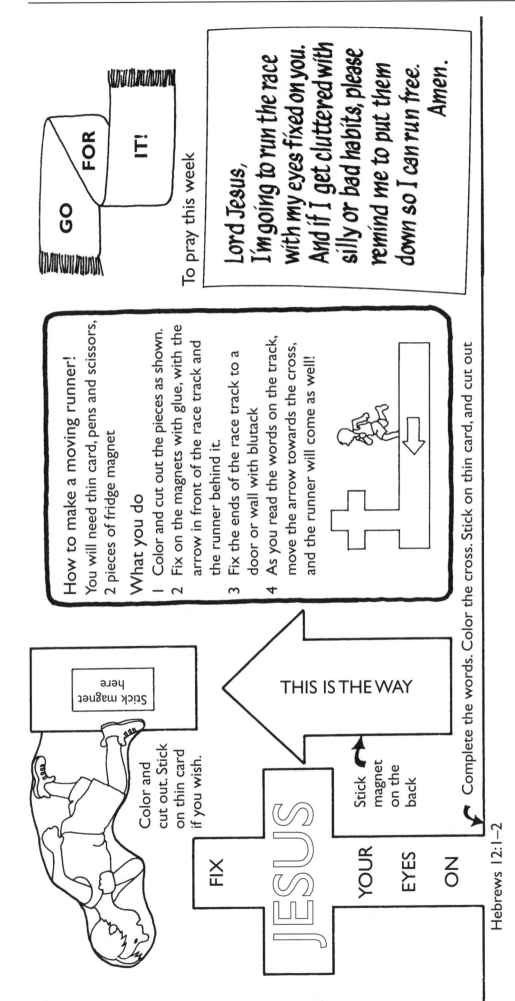

THIS IS THE WAY

Stick magnet on the back

Stick magnet here

Color and cut out. Stick on thin card if you wish.

FIX
JESUS
YOUR
EYES
ON

Hebrews 12:1–2

WE SHOULD T _ _ _ _ OFF EVERYTHING THAT H _ _ _ _ _ _ _ US, ESPECIALLY THE

S _ _ THAT C _ _ _ _ SO EASILY, AND KEEP R _ _ _ _ _ STEADILY IN THE

R _ _ _ WE HAVE S _ _ _ _ _ . LET US NOT LOSE S _ _ _ _ OF J _ _ _ _ .

Twenty-first Sunday in Ordinary Time

Thought for the day

At the great and final gathering-in, it will be a question of each person's chosen life direction, and each response to the way of God.

Readings

Isaiah 66:18–21
Hebrews 12:5–7, 11–13
Luke 13:22–30

Aim: To be introduced to Jesus' teaching about the narrow door, and the way to eternal life.

Starter

Give out needles and thread, and see who is the fastest at threading a needle. Now try with yarn and see if anyone can manage it. Or they could try squashing a sleeping bag into its sack.

Teaching

Beforehand prepare a narrow gateway, perhaps from two chairs with tall cardboard against them, or two leaders standing back to back. You'll also need some bulky parcels such as rolled sleeping bags, huge balloons, large cartons tied with string and so on.

Explain that Jesus was always wanting to help people understand about the important things like life and death, and why we are alive, and what happens when we die. All humans wonder about these things. Jesus could see that some people obviously thought they were definitely going to be okay when they died because they were Jewish and part of God's chosen people. Jesus wanted to show them that we can't earn a place in heaven by working hard, and we can't buy a ticket for it either. This is how Jesus explained it.

He said that getting to heaven is rather like having to go through a very narrow gate. We've just been finding out how hard it is to get a thick piece of yarn or string through a narrow needle, and a huge sleeping bag through the narrow opening of its sack.

Load a volunteer up with all the bulky parcels and explain that our problem with getting through a narrow gate is all the baggage we carry with us. We carry bags of "I want," parcels of "doubt," sacks of "I've got to be better than anyone else" and boxes of "I love me." (The volunteer can demonstrate how hard it is to get through the narrow gate with this lot.)

What Jesus was saying was that entering the everlasting happiness of heaven is like going through a narrow gate because we just can't take any of this luggage with us. All God wants is for us to be ourselves, honestly and humbly trusting Jesus. Then it doesn't matter that the gate is narrow because we're not trying to get our cool image through with us, or any of the other things. None of us deserves a place in heaven; we can only receive it as a free gift from the Jesus we know and love. And he will give us that gift when he recognizes us.

Praying

Lord Jesus, I want you to recognize me
as one of your followers.
Give me the courage to follow you
and learn from you about real loving.
Amen.

Activities

On the activity sheet there is a wordsearch for key-words of today's teaching, and a model to make of the narrow gate. The children will need soft modeling clay (like plasticine) to make the person and all the bags.

Notes

R	Y	A	V	S	H	L	D	K	M
E	L	R	N	A	R	R	O	W	L
C	H	W	G	I	B	T	O	N	O
O	S	I	Q	F	B	H	R	J	V
G	I	L	H	J	P	T	O	N	I
N	F	L	C	A	G	E	I	O	N
I	L	G	O	D	R	A	S	T	G
Z	E	P	F	U	Z	D	N	S	L
E	S	S	C	D	M	P	T	R	Y
K	U	Y	W	O	R	D	E	Q	L

Jesus said, 'TRY HARD to enter through the NARROW DOOR.' GOD WILL NOT RECOGNIZE US if we have spent our lives SELFISHLY instead of LOVINGLY.

To pray this week

Lord Jesus,
I want you to recognise me as one of your followers. Give me the courage to follow you and learn from you about real loving.　Amen.

Make a model person this big

Press the baggage on to the model person and they can't get through the narrow door. Take them off and the person CAN get through.

and some bulky bags this big . . .

I WANT

I LOVE ME

I'VE GOT TO BE BETTER THAN ANYONE ELSE

ENTER

CUT

KINGDOM OF HEAVEN

FOLD

CUT

FOLD

FOLD

CUT

FOLD

'Yes, I know you. Welcome to the kingdom of heaven'

ALL SELFISHNESS MUST BE LEFT AT THE DOOR

Twenty-second Sunday in Ordinary Time

Thought for the day

When we live God's way, both individually and as a community, we will be greatly blessed.

Readings

Sirach 3:17–18, 20, 28–29
Hebrews 12:18–19, 22–24
Luke 14:1, 7–14

Aim: To look at the implications of Jesus' teaching about hospitality.

Starter

In pairs, feed one another with spoonfuls of water. Provide clothing protection!

Teaching

Beforehand prepare two children to act out the guests at the party who are taking the top and bottom seats, and have to swap round when the host wants the lower one up at the top.

Talk about the way we usually feed ourselves when we're hungry, and give ourselves drinks when we're thirsty. When we were feeding one another we got an idea of what it's like to look after someone else, checking that they have caught the spoonful, and don't have drips down their chin.

Thinking of other people's needs is an important part of the Christian way of living. One day Jesus was invited out to lunch, and he noticed the pushy way some of the guests were making sure they had the best seats, nearest the food and drink and near the hosts, so sitting there would make them look important. Jesus didn't like what he saw. It made him sad that people were pushy like this, wanting to be more important than anyone else, and not thinking of other people's feelings. So he told them this story to help them understand a better way of living.

Now ask the children to perform the sketch they have prepared, with the rest of the children being the rest of the guests. Draw out the point Jesus was making about wrong values—being thought of as important shouldn't matter to us nearly as much as it often does. As Christians we are not to think "What's in this for me?" all the time.

Praying

Jesus, teach me to give
and not to count the cost,
to toil and not to seek for rest,
to work and not to ask for any reward
except the reward of knowing
I am doing your will. Amen.

Activities

The activity sheet encourages the children to look at the second part of today's teaching, dealing with our hospitality with no strings attached. There are also recipes and suggestions for staging a party, with an invitation format, so that they can put the teaching straight into practice as part of your parish outreach program.

Notes

Who are we to invite?

those who are not usually invited anywhere

those who can't invite you back

just those who will buy you a big present

just those who will ask you back

NO

NO

YES

YES

To pray this week

Jesus, teach me to give and not to count the cost, to toil and not to seek for rest, to work and not to ask for any reward except the reward of knowing I am doing your will.   Amen.

Why not throw a party?

Banana milkshake

You will need

half a pint of milk

a banana

teaspoon of runny honey

What you do
Peel and chop the banana.
Put everything in a screw-top jar.
Shake it lots.
Pour into a glass.

dips and dishes

sticks of carrot and cucumber

hollow pepper

dice cakes
chocolate pieces and a slab of cake cut up and covered in white icing

PARTY TIME

yogurt, mayonnaise and chopped chives

tomato
sliced olives
sliced red pepper
cheese
peppers

crunchies
cornflakes stuck together with chocolate

pizza faces

Dear ....
Please will you come to
a party at ...., held at
on ....
....
Love from .... RSVP

Twenty-third Sunday in Ordinary Time

Thought for the day

Following Jesus is expensive—it costs everything, but it's worth it.

Readings

Wisdom 9:13–18
Philemon 9–10, 12–17
Luke 14:25–33

Aim: To look at what it costs to follow Jesus.

Starter

Tower building. Collect lots of boxes and cartons, and sort them into sizes with price tags on them. Use Monopoly money and make the prices of the "bricks" very high, so the children are dealing in hundreds of dollars. Issue each small group with a set amount of money and have a leader in charge of the brickyard. The members of the teams have to decide which bricks to buy with their money to stack up their tower.

Teaching

Use two leaders or a leader and a child to tell the story as a conversation, something like this:

> *Miriam is sweeping the floor when Alex comes bursting in.*

Alex   Miriam! Miriam! Where are you? Oh, there you are!

Miriam   Now, watch where you put the dust from those sandals, Alex. I've just swept over there!

Alex   Oh, yes…sorry, dear. But listen, I've had a *really* good idea.

Miriam   Not another one already! I was cleaning up after your last good idea for days.

Alex   Ah, the olive tree shaker, you mean. Well, I wasn't to know the olives and insects would all shake off into your bowl of flour, was I! Anyway, this idea is different, and it's *really good.*

Miriam   OK, dear, I'm listening. You do have some very good ideas, I know. You just need someone like me to keep you from getting carried away, sometimes. Tell me your idea.

Alex   A tower.

Miriam   A tower? What do you mean, a tower?

Alex   I'm going to build one! It'll be very high, so you'll be able to climb up the tower and check on all the sheep and lambs without having to go all the way to the fields! There, what do you think?

Miriam   Mmm, it sounds like a good time-saver. I could sit at the top of your tower and sunbathe in between looking at the sheep, couldn't I?

Alex   Yes, Miriam, you could.

Miriam   There's one rather big problem though.

Alex   Oh, really? What's that, Miriam?

Miriam   Money. Bricks cost money, and we haven't got any spare money that I know of. How are you going to pay for it?

Alex   Well, I've got enough bricks to build the first part, Miriam.

Miriam   Oh, Alex, you'll like look a prize idiot if you build the first part and then can't finish it! All the neighbors would tease you about it for years.

Alex   Yes, I suppose you're right. Perhaps I'll go and sit under the olive tree before supper and think it over.

Miriam   It's chicken soup and dumplings, and I'll need some help!

Then read Luke 14:28–30, 33. If we decide to join Cubs or Brownies, or start a new sport or learn to play the flute, we know we are committing ourselves. We know our choice will take up time, and we won't be able to do some other things.

Following Jesus is a commitment, too. We have to be prepared to work at telling the truth, or getting along with people we find difficult, or standing up for what is right even when we get teased for it. We can't follow Jesus and go on cheating and lying as if nothing has changed. We have to be prepared to put down those bad habits we have gotten into and Jesus will help us in that. We have to be ready to go wherever Jesus leads us; and that could be any-where.

Praying

Lord, even before I say a word,
you already know what I am going to say.
You are all around me—in front and at the back.
You have put your hand on me.
Your knowledge is amazing to me.
It is more than I can understand.

(From Psalm 139)

Activities

There is a cost-counting puzzle on the activity sheet, and the instructions for making a reversible cross which looks at the cost and the benefits of following Christ.

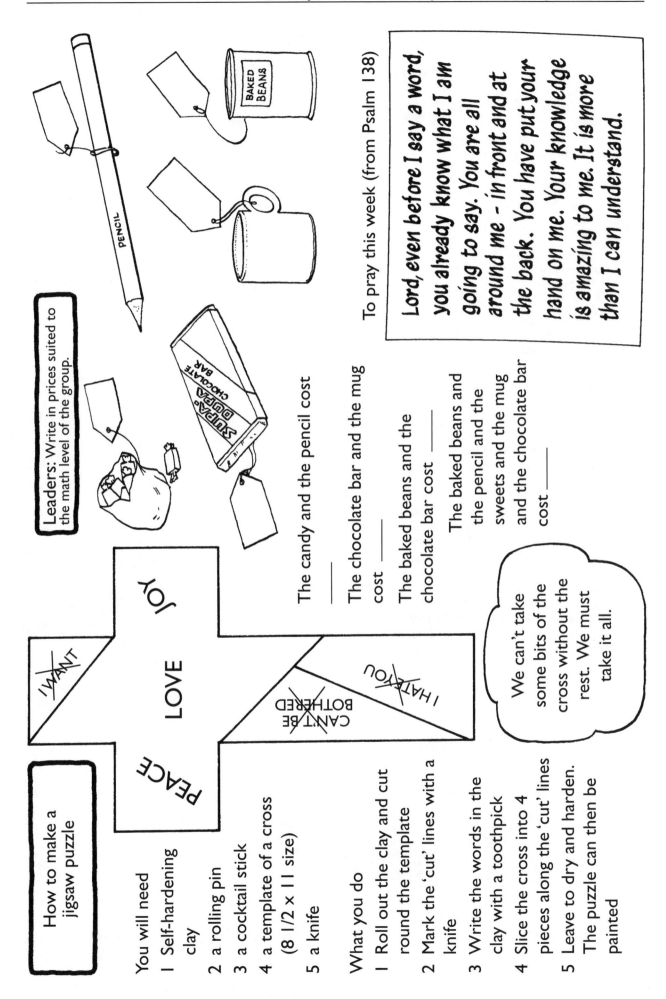

PENCIL

BAKED BEANS

SUPA DUPA CHOCOLATE BAR

Leaders: Write in prices suited to the math level of the group.

To pray this week (from Psalm 138)

Lord, even before I say a word, you already know what I am going to say. You are all around me – in front and at the back. You have put your hand on me. Your knowledge is amazing to me. It is more than I can understand.

The candy and the pencil cost ____

The chocolate bar and the mug cost ____

The baked beans and the chocolate bar cost ____

The baked beans and the pencil and the sweets and the mug and the chocolate bar cost ____

We can't take some bits of the cross without the rest. We must take it all.

JOY
I WANT
LOVE
I HATE YOU
CAN'T BE BOTHERED
PEACE

How to make a jigsaw puzzle

You will need

1 Self-hardening clay
2 a rolling pin
3 a cocktail stick
4 a template of a cross (8 1/2 × 11 size)
5 a knife

What you do

1 Roll out the clay and cut round the template
2 Mark the 'cut' lines with a knife
3 Write the words in the clay with a toothpick
4 Slice the cross into 4 pieces along the 'cut' lines
5 Leave to dry and harden. The puzzle can then be painted

Twenty-fourth Sunday in Ordinary Time

Thought for the day

Jesus does not avoid the company of sinners but befriends them.

Readings

Exodus 32:7–11, 13–14
1 Timothy 1:12–17
Luke 15:1–32

Aim: To explore the meaning of the lost sheep and the lost coin.

Starter

Hunt the coins. Have larger groups hunt several coins at the same time.

Teaching

Share your stories of losing something really important and then finding it again after searching everywhere for it. (Or you could pretend to have lost something and get everyone searching for it. When it is found you can draw attention to the relief and happiness.)

Jesus knew what this was like. Perhaps it was his mom or aunt who had once lost one of those coins from a marriage necklace, and he remembered the way they had all searched and celebrated.

Show the children a picture of such a necklace, or, if possible, a real example borrowed from your local Resource center, and tell the story of the woman losing one of the coins. Use a real broom as you describe the sweeping of the whole house.

Explain that whenever one of us gets "lost"— cut off from God—he too is really sad, and keeps searching and searching until he finds us again.

Praying

We pray for those
who have made wrong choices
and cut themselves off from God.
We pray for all those
who are living evil lives.
May all the lost be found again. Amen.

Activities

There are instructions on the activity sheet for making a marriage necklace and a sheep, and a puzzle to reinforce the two stories of the sheep and the coin.

Luke 15 verse 10

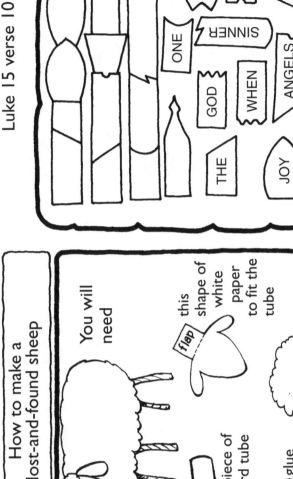

HEART
AMONG
HIS
IS
CHANGES
ONE
SINNER
GOD
WHEN
ANGELS
OF
THE
JOY
THERE

To pray this week

We pray for those who have made wrong choices and cut themselves off from God. We pray for all those who are living evil lives. May all the lost be found again.   *Amen.*

How to make a lost-and-found sheep

You will need

flap — this shape of white paper to fit the tube

sheep's wool or cotton wool

a piece of card tube

glue

2 pipe cleaners

What you do

Draw the face on and stick the flap inside the tube.

Make 4 holes in the bottom of the tube and thread the pipe cleaners through.

Stick wool on the tube and the top of the face.

You can hide your sheep and get your friend to find it.

How to make a headband dowry of shiny coins

You will need

gold and silver wrapping paper/foil

circles of thin card

cotton   needle or stapler

glue

a band of material (from an old sheet, perhaps) to fit round your head.

What you do

1 Cut round the card circles on the paper and stick the paper to the card.

2 Sew the band of material into a circle that fits your head.

3 Sew the coins on to the front of the band, or staple them.

4 Put on the band and wear a head-scarf as shown.

Twenty-fifth Sunday in Ordinary Time

Thought for the day

If you cannot be trusted with worldly riches, or even small amounts of money, then you will not be trusted with spiritual riches either.

Readings

Amos 8:4–7
1 Timothy 2:1–8
Luke 16:1–13

Aim: To get to know the story of the clever manager, and explore its meaning.

Starter

Who's in charge? One person goes outside the room. The others decide on a leader. Everyone stands in a circle and copies the leader's actions, while the person who was outside tries to guess who the leader is.

Teaching

Today we are going to hear a story Jesus told about someone who was put in charge, and got into a bit of trouble.

If possible, use a few costume items, such as a suit jacket for the manager, Hawaiian shirt and shades for the rich man, a large accounts book, a plastic bottle of olive oil, and a bag of flour. First the rich man interviews the manager and gives him the job. They shake hands and the rich man leaves the manager to sort out the accounts. The manager thinks aloud, casually helping himself to the petty cash, and writing it in as expenses. He makes a careful job of forging the rich man's signature on large checks, pleased that his cheating is going so well, and priding himself on all his skill and hard work at making money like this.

Then the rich man comes in, waving a check and saying his bank manager has just shown it to him. He demands a full report and fires the manager. On his own again, the manager makes his plans to ensure he'll be well looked after once he is without a job. He can go to different children and ask them what they owe, looking in his book and saying, "Now let's see—you owe 3,000 liters of olive oil/ 36,000 liters of flour, I believe?"

The rich man can be creeping behind him, watching what he is doing. As the manager turns around after the last transaction, he bumps into the rich man, and starts pretending he's been checking up on this person's old mother (or some other con story). The rich man stops him and says he's seen

everything. He shakes his hand and laughs, saying something like, "Well, you're a terrible rogue, and I wouldn't trust you as far as I can jump, but you certainly work hard at it!"

When Jesus told this story, he said that we all know crooks work really hard cheating people out of their money to get rich; it's a pity that we don't work as hard at getting rich with God's treasures! If we put as much energy into our caring love as that crooked manager put into his cheating, the world would be a much more loving place.

Praying

Dear God,
help us to work hard
at good things
like loving and sharing,
and not to work hard
at bad things
like lying and cheating. Amen.

Activities

On the activity sheet there is a blotted page of the accounts book for them to put right, and a checklist of the things in life they work hardest at. They are encouraged to look at the way they spend their pocket money, and to think about giving some away each week to help someone else. Organizations like Catholic Relief Services have children's packs with suggestions for cooperative giving which you could consider.

Notes

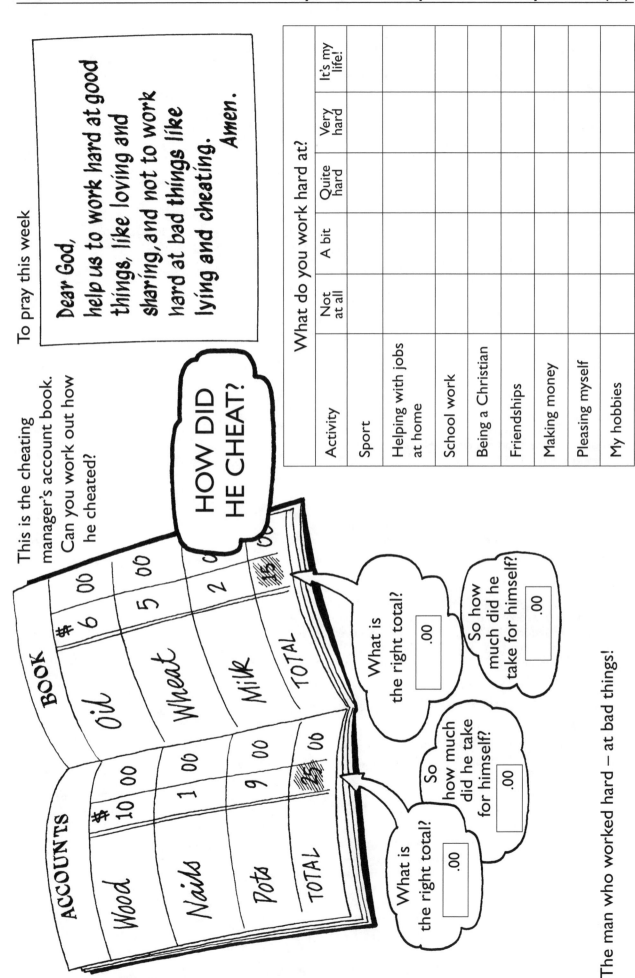

To pray this week

Dear God,
help us to work hard at good things, like loving and sharing, and not to work hard at bad things like lying and cheating. **Amen.**

This is the cheating manager's account book. Can you work out how he cheated?

HOW DID HE CHEAT?

What do you work hard at?

Activity	Not at all	A bit	Quite hard	Very hard	It's my life!
Sport					
Helping with jobs at home					
School work					
Being a Christian					
Friendships					
Making money					
Pleasing myself					
My hobbies					

ACCOUNTS BOOK

	#	
Wood	10	00
Nails	1	00
Pots	9	00
TOTAL	25	00

	#	
Oil	6	00
Wheat	5	00
Milk	2	00
TOTAL	15	00

What is the right total? ____ .00

So how much did he take for himself? ____ .00

What is the right total? ____ .00

So how much did he take for himself? ____ .00

The man who worked hard — at bad things!

Twenty-sixth Sunday in Ordinary Time

Thought for the day

Wealth can make us complacent so that we fail to notice the needs of those around us.

Readings

Amos 6:1a, 4–7
1 Timothy 6:11–16
Luke 16:19–31

Aim: To get to know the story of the rich man and Lazarus.

Starter

During a song, arrange for one of the leaders to come in wearing a hat and carrying a trowel, walk across the room and go out again. Don't draw attention to this; ignore it. After the song, ask the children if they noticed anyone coming in during the song, and what they looked like. The person comes in again, and explains that today we are going to hear about someone who didn't take any notice of the needs of someone he saw every day.

Teaching

Use the children to be Lazarus and the rich man, the dogs, the angels and Abraham, as you narrate the story, either directly from the Bible (the *New Century Children's International Bible* is excellent) or in your own words. If you have a spare leader you can go for voice-overs as well.

After the story, talk about what the rich man had done wrong, and how his wealth had made him so comfortable that he didn't notice the needs of others staring him in the face. The children may have some ideas of how the rich man could have done it better.

Praying

Lord, we pray for the poor
and those who don't have enough to eat.
We give you ourselves
for you to use
in helping them. Amen.

Activities

On the activity sheet they can confirm their commitment to put their faith into practice by drawing someone they can help, and how they plan to do it.

Notes

L	A	Z	A	R	U	S	C	H	U
S	B	A	R	I	T	G	O	O	B
X	R	I	C	C	N	O	M	S	E
G	A	Q	A	H	K	D	F	I	G
B	H	F	B	N	M	E	O	G	G
J	A	T	D	M	G	F	R	U	I
R	M	C	G	A	T	E	T	M	N
Z	L	A	V	N	J	W	L	P	G
Q	K	O	D	H	L	E	Y	S	N
S	U	F	F	E	R	I	N	G	P

Luke 16:19–31

LAZARUS   DOGS
RICH MAN   ANGELS
GATE   ABRAHAM
BEGGING   COMFORT
               SUFFERING

Use the words to remind
you of the story

I want to help

This is how I will help them

To pray this week

Lord, we pray for the poor
and those who don't have
enough to eat.
We give you ourselves for
you to use in helping them.
            Amen.

Twenty-seventh Sunday in Ordinary Time

Thought for the day
God hears our distress and our crying, and feels it with us.

Readings
Habakkuk 1:2–3; 2:2–4
2 Timothy 1:6–8, 13–14
Luke 17:5–10

Aim: To get to know the parable of the servant doing his duty.

Starter
Put on some music, and do a challenging fitness workout, including, perhaps, running on the spot, stepping, skipping, bunny jumps, stretching, and touching toes. Praise them for the way they kept going and kept trying, even when it was hard or tiring.

Teaching
Like our fitness training session, life can sometimes be hard work—such as when we feel jealous of a brother or sister, or when we are finding it difficult to do the work at school, or when there are arguments and rows at home. Collect their ideas and experiences.

How does our God help us at these times, and what tips has Jesus got for coping?

Use simple puppets to act out the story that Jesus told about the servant, doing it the first time with the servant coming in and putting his feet up, and the master protesting that he can't behave like that because he's a servant, not the master. Then make a "take two" sign and act the situation out with the servant being praised at the end for doing all the jobs. The servant can then protest that he was only doing his duty.

What does the story mean? Jesus says that we are not to expect life to be easy and perfect all the time because it isn't. We can expect there to be sad and difficult times as well as all the happy and easy times. And when they happen, we are to just carry on doing what we know is right, without grumbling too much. God will be there with us in all the difficult times, so we won't be left alone, and he will give us the strength we need to carry on.

Praying
Set out a train layout, with a tunnel (which can be a shoe box with holes at the ends), a gradient and some points. Start the train around the track as you pray:

When life seems an uphill struggle, Lord,
All: keep me on track with you, Jesus.

When we go through dark and lonely times,
All: keep me on track with you, Jesus.

When we have to make choices about how to behave,
All: keep me on track with you, Jesus. Amen.

Activities
There are instructions on the activity sheet for making a "spinner" to remind them of the need to persevere when times are hard, and there is a Bible study activity for which they will need Bibles.

Notes

Code key

A	C	D	E	F	G	I	L	N	O	P	R	S	T	U	V	W

2 Timothy 1:6-8

This letter was written by .... Paul wants Timothy

to .... Paul wants Timothy

to .... into a .... the

gift that God gave him.

HOW TO MAKE A SPINNER

1 Color the spinner and cut it out.

2 Stick it on to thin card.

3 Poke a toothpick through the middle.

As your spinner spins, it can remind you to go on and on praying, trusting and loving

To pray this week

When life seems an uphill struggle, Lord, keep me on track with you, Jesus. When we go through dark and lonely times, keep me on track with you, Jesus. When we have to make choices about how to behave, keep me on track with you, Jesus.
Amen.

KEEP ON TRUSTING · KEEP ON LOVING · KEEP ON PRAYING

Twenty-eighth Sunday in Ordinary Time

Thought for the day
God can always use even seemingly hopeless situations for good.

Readings
2 Kings 5:14–17
2 Timothy 2:8–13
Luke 17:11–19

Aim: To look at the healing of the lepers and the significance of the one who said "thank you."

Starter
Musical chairs, or a similar game, where there is always an odd one out when the music stops. Today we are going to think about ten odd ones out, and one odd one out.

Teaching
Two mothers, dressed up in turbans, are in a village with their pots, collecting water from the village well. They pass the time of day, and then catch sight of the ten lepers in the distance, wondering who they are shouting to. One of the lepers, Jonas, is the son of one of the women and they talk about how sad they are that he can't live at home anymore, and how badly he is missed, and how they have never stopped praying for him to be healed. They see that Jesus, the healer and teacher, is coming toward their village, and has stopped to listen to the lepers.

They wonder if Jesus could possibly be making the lepers better. They watch the lepers running away from Jesus and suddenly realize they are heading for the priest's house and are throwing off their bandages as they run. The women get very excited and soon they see some of the lepers running into their own houses in the village. They must be healed! The women start praising God, and are looking forward to Jonas coming back when they see him running all on his own back up the road to Jesus. What on earth is he doing? Then they see Jonas kneel down in front of Jesus. He is pouring out his thanks to Jesus, who is smiling and sharing Jonas's delight. The two women pick up their pots of water and go off to join them.

Praying
Put up all ten fingers and lower the fingers one by one as you say the first ten words. As you say "Thank you!" you make a thumbs-up sign with one thumb, representing the thankful leper.

You always make us feel better.
Help us to say, "Thank you!"

Activities
The activity sheet gives instructions for making a pop-up thank-you card. There is also a puzzle for which they will need access to a Bible. This reinforces the week's teaching.

Notes

How to make a pop-up card

You will need

glue

colored paper

pens

scissors

What you do

1 Color the pop-up 'thank you' in bright colors
2 Fold it down the middle
3 Fold the colored paper down the middle
4 Stick the side edges of the pop-up 'thank you' to each side of the card.

stick

stick

fold

stick

THANK YOU!

To pray this week

1 You
2 always
3 make
4 us
5 feel
6 better.
7 Help
8 us
9 to
10 say

'THANK YOU!'

THANK YOU!

J ① was ② his way to a v ③ when he met ④ lepers. They asked him to h ⑤ pity on them. Jesus healed all ten of them but o ⑥ o ⑦ of them came b ⑧ to say ' ⑨ !'

Luke 17:11-19

Twenty-ninth Sunday in Ordinary Time

Thought for the day
Don't get side-tracked; always pray and don't give up.

Readings
Exodus 17:8–13
2 Timothy 3:14—4:2
Luke 18:1–8

Aim: To learn about perseverance in prayer and Scripture-reading.

Starter
Sit in a circle. You start by saying, "Every morning I say my prayers." Everyone in turn adds something else to the list of what they do each morning, and repeats all the things that have been already mentioned. This ensures that everyone voices the prayer activity. Also, the separate letters for "Prayer" and "Scripture-reading" (different colors for each) are hidden around the room, and the children sent to hunt them out. They persevere until they have all the letters and can sort them out into the words.

Teaching
Use the sketch from the All-age ideas to introduce the parable of the woman pestering the judge for her rights, and then talk about why they think Jesus told this story.

Woman	Knock, knock.
Judge	Who's there?
Woman	Winnie.
Judge	Winnie who?
Woman	Winnie you going to do something about that money I was cheated out of?
Judge	Oh don't worry, that case will be coming up very soon. Now if you don't mind, it's my day off and I'm going to play golf.
	(Sign held up saying "Next day")
Woman	Knock, knock.
Judge	Who's there?
Woman	Winnie.
Judge	Winnie who?
Woman	Winnie you going to do something about …
Judge	OK, you don't have to say all that again.

I remember. I'll deal with it, madam. Leave it to me. *(Aside)* But not yet because I'd rather watch television and have a snooze.

Woman	Knock, knock.
Judge	*(Sounding sleepy)* Who's there?
Woman	Winnie.
Judge	Winnie who? *(Aside)* Oh, hang on, I won't ask! I don't know, there's no rest for the wicked. Wretched woman, I'd better do what she asks or I'll never get any peace! *(Shouts)* All right, Winnie, you win. I'll come with you and sort it out *now*!

What is the story saying to us? Point out that Jesus was saying, "If even a lazy old judge like that eventually listened to the woman, we can be certain that our loving God will listen to us right away every time, and answer our prayer." Sometimes his answer might be that we have to wait, or that what we are asking for wouldn't help us forward as much as we think it would.

Have an alarm clock, a knife and fork and spoon, a musical box lullaby, and a toothbrush and toothpaste.

Set them down and talk about these as being the times to remember to pray, so that we are sure to be praying at least at these times. It doesn't have to take hours, but we do need to make contact with God several times each day. Put a praying logo next to all of the items, and an open Bible in front of them, asking them to think of the best time for them to do this.

Show them some suitable daily Scripture-reading aids and invite parents to look at some Bible translations you recommend.

Praying
Use the symbols from the teaching.

Lord God, I want to keep in touch with you
all through the day.
Help me to remember that in the morning
    (ring the alarm)
before I eat
    (clash the knife and fork)
and before I go to sleep
    (play the lullaby or brush teeth)
I can talk to you and know you are listening.

Activities
The activity sheet helps them make a week's chart to set them off on the praying and Scripture-reading habit, for which they can be rewarded next week.

See how quickly you can find these verses and read them

Genesis 1:1–2

Exodus 14:21–22

Luke 2:6–7

1 Samuel 17:48–49

Matthew 9:23–25

Mark 15:25–26

John 20:19–20

Psalm 23:1–2

To pray this week

Lord God, I want to keep in touch with you all through the day. Help me to remember that in the morning before I eat and before I go to sleep I can talk to you and know you are listening.

All completed charts get a prize!

Luke 18 1–8

This is the name of the book

18 This is the chapter

1–8 These are the verses

COMPETITION TIME
Start a good habit!

1 Cut out and fold into a stand-up zig-zag. Write your name on the back.

2 As you pray and read your Bible each day this week color in the logos

3 Bring it back next week, signed by Mom, Dad or the person who looks after you

MONDAY	TUESDAY	WEDNESDAY	THURSDAY	FRIDAY	SATURDAY
Signed	Signed	Signed	Signed	Signed	Signed

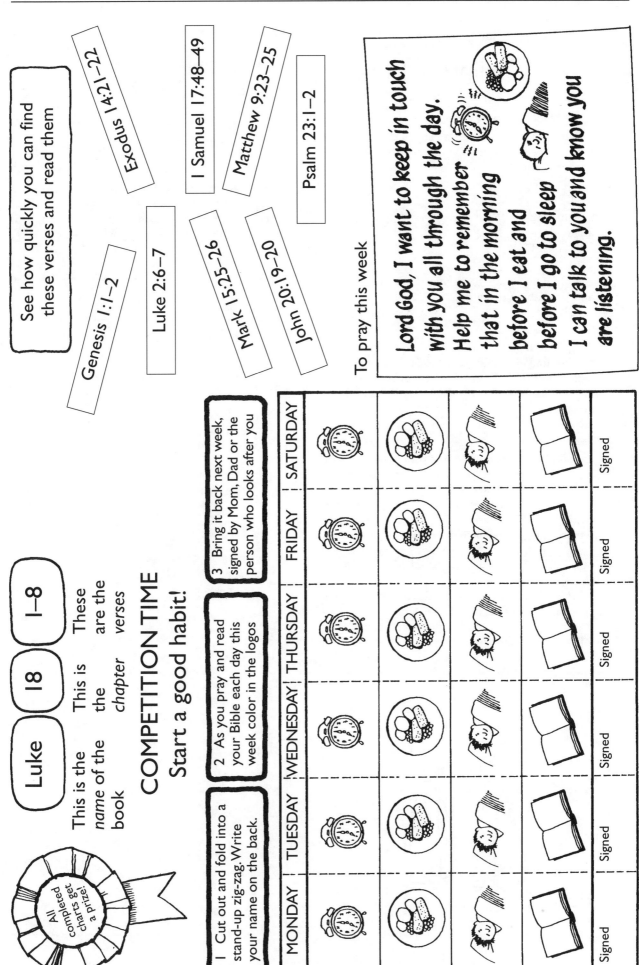

Thirtieth Sunday in Ordinary Time

Thought for the day

When we recognize our dependence on God we will approach him with true humility and accept his gifts with joy.

Readings

Sirach 35:12–14, 16–18
2 Timothy 4:6–8, 16–18
Luke 18:9–14

Aim: To get to know the parable from Luke 18:9–14 and learn about being right with God.

Starter

A "getting it right" game, such as pinning the tail on the donkey (blindfolded), or using marbles or dice to roll on to a board with numbered squares on it. The number your marble or dice lands on is your score.

Teaching

Explain that Jesus found some people he was with were always looking down on others, and acting like they were much better than everyone else. They seemed to have forgotten that they owed their whole life to God. Jesus didn't like to see that, and it made him sad. So he told them this story to show them how they were behaving, hoping it would make them realize what they were doing and try to change.

Use simple puppets, made out of wooden spoons or spatulas, to tell the story. The pictures below will help you with the expressions. Then talk about which one of the two went home right with God, and why. Reinforce that we all depend on God for our life, and everything comes from him.

Praying

You know us, Lord,
so we can't pretend with you.
You shower us with blessings
like a shower of rain;
you give us your power
to make us grow more loving
all through our lives.

Activities

Using the activity sheet the children can make their own puppets. With these they can use the script provided, which reinforces our need to be in a right position with God, knowing our dependence on him.

Notes

Jesus Come down, Zacchaeus! I'm coming to tea with you today.

Zacchaeus Tea with me? Are you sure? I'm not a very good person, you know.

Jesus I know that. But you could be a very kind person and I think you would like to be kind.

Zacchaeus You're right, Jesus. I don't like being mean and cheating people.

Jesus God can help you to change.

Zacchaeus Oh wow! I'm going to be generous and kind from today!

To pray this week

You know us, Lord, so we can't pretend with you. You shower us with blessings like a shower of rain; You give us your power to make us grow more loving all through our lives.

Make the puppets and they can talk together . . .

Tape a pencil or stick on the back to make your puppets

Zacchaeus

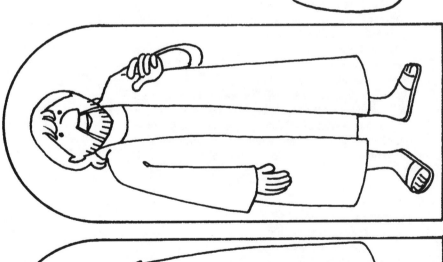

Jesus

Color in the puppets and cut them out

Luke 19:1-10

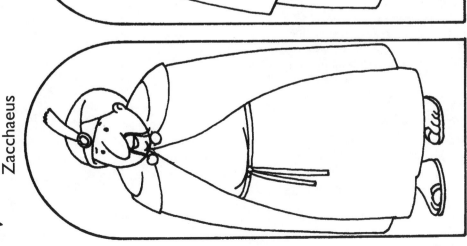

Thirty-first Sunday in Ordinary Time

Thought for the day

Jesus came to search out the lost and save them. Through him we come to our senses and make our lives clean.

Readings

Wisdom 11:22—12:2
2 Thessalonians 1:11—2:2
Luke 19:1–10

Aim: To learn about the fun of being forgiven and having a fresh start.

Starter

Bring a selection of chalkboards, chalk and dampened cloths, magic slates (which let you erase what you have written), white board, pens and cleaning cloth, and sand trays. Have a time of free play with these, so they can enjoy the satisfaction of drawing and erasing and starting again.

Teaching

Talk about what they have been doing, and the fun of being able to start again whenever you make a mistake. Sometimes we make mistakes and do things that are wrong, and we wish they could be rubbed out as well as our drawings today.

Well, with Jesus, they can! Today we are going to hear about someone who met Jesus and was able to make a completely fresh start.

Tell the story of Zacchaeus using cut-out pictures on a background of carpet squares or towels. The children can help place the houses and trees, and the crowd of people. As you tell the story, get the children to imagine what the other people were thinking when Jesus noticed the cheating tax collector, what Zacchaeus was thinking when he was noticed, and how he felt when he made a fresh start.

Praying

Lord my God,
you and I both know
the mistakes I make in life.
Please rub them out for me,
and forgive me all my sins
so that I can make a fresh start,
starting today.

Activities

On the activity sheet there are instructions for making a tree with Zacchaeus in it (using a flap), and a cartoon story to remind them of how good it feels to be forgiven and start fresh.

Color the tree and the flap. Fold the flap and push through the slit

1. Oliver wanted to be in the gang. "You can't be in it unless you steal some sweets" they said.

2. After school Oliver went to the sweet shop. He managed to steal a Mars bar, without the shopkeeper seeing.

3. They let him join the gang. Oliver was proud to be in. But he kept feeling bad about the stealing.

4. He worried about it in bed and at school. He knew it was wrong and he kept pretending it was OK to steal.

5. At last he told his Dad. It felt so good to have got rid of the worry. Dad went with him to the shop and he paid for the Mars bar. He felt HAPPY !!

Tim has rubbed out his mistakes. Can you draw in the bits he got wrong?

Zacchaeus! Hu up and come dc

To pray together

Lord my God, you and I both know the mistakes I make in life. Please rub them out for me, and forgive me all my sins so that I can make a fresh start, starting today!

Thirty-second Sunday in Ordinary Time

Thought for the day

Life after death is not wishful thinking but a definite reality.

Readings

2 Maccabees 7:1–2, 9–14
2 Thessalonians 2:16—3:5
Luke 20:27–38

Aim: To stretch our minds to imagine things beyond our physical sight.

Starter

Put on some praise music, and do lots of stretching exercises to the music.

Teaching

Explain that we have been stretching our bodies and now we are going to stretch our minds as well. (Don't rush this journey—shut your own eyes and actually imagine it as you direct them and that will get the timing right.) Get them to shut their eyes and imagine their town all around them...and beyond that all the countryside stretching out to the sea all around them...imagine the round world curving away from where they are sitting so they are riding on the ball-shaped planet earth through space, going slowly round the brilliant sun. Take them on a speeded-up reverse journey to end up back in your hall or class, where they can open their eyes.

Even though we don't usually think about it or imagine it, we are actually doing that journey all the time! We really are perched on the outside of a planet, riding through space around the sun.

Jesus liked to get people to stretch their minds. There is so much that we can't see because it's too huge, or too minute, or simply invisible. We can't see heaven but Jesus told his friends that there definitely is life after death, and when we die we will know exactly what it is like.

For the moment, though, while we live bound by things like time and space, we can only imagine how wonderful and brilliant heaven will be.

Some people, both now and then, didn't believe in life after death. They came to Jesus and asked him a tricky question. (You can either use children or lego-type people for this.)

There was this woman (choose a girl to stand up) and she got married (choose a boy to stand). Then the husband died (boy falls down) so she married someone else (another boy stands up)...

Carry on for seven husbands. Now at the resurrection (all the dead husbands stand up again), to whom is the woman going to be married? (The girl pretends to look very puzzled.)

Let everyone sit down again. The people asking the question thought Jesus would have to agree that life after death was a silly idea. But he didn't. Jesus told them that they were expecting life in heaven to carry on in just the same way as life on earth, but it's not like that. In heaven there won't be things like who's married to whom because we will be like angels, just happy to be God's children.

Praying

And our eyes at last shall see him
through his own redeeming love.
For that child, so dear and gentle,
is our Lord in heaven above.
And he leads his children on
to the place where he is gone.

Activities

On the activity sheet there are some examples of the "tasters" of heaven we are given on earth, and space for them to include others. There are also some mind-stretching puzzles.

Notes

LIFE after DEATH is

just made up

the real truth

wishful thinking

NO

NO

YES

knowing God loves you

enjoying lovely things

being happy for other people

feeling forgiven

'Tastes' of heaven

Add your own ideas

To pray this week

And our eyes at last shall see him through his own redeeming love. For that child, so dear and gentle, is our Lord in heaven above. And he leads his children on to the place where he is gone.

If you had had climbed the tree what would you see?

If you looked at this through a magnifying glass, what would you see?

Thirty-third Sunday in Ordinary Time

Thought for the day

There will be dark and dangerous times as the end approaches, but by standing firm through it all we will gain life.

Readings

Malachi 3:19–20
2 Thessalonians 3:7–12
Luke 21:5–19

Aim: To know that standing firm to the end is hard but worthwhile.

Starter

No yes, no no. Try to answer everyone's questions without using the words "yes" and "no."

Teaching

Look at some examples of signs that tell us about things that are going to happen, like posters to advertise plays and concerts, road signs, weather signs (such as "red sky at night, shepherds' delight," and cloud formations) and illness signs (such as feeling hot and shaky, or having a rash).

Today we are going to hear about the signs which Jesus said would mark the coming of the last age before all things are completed at the end of time.

Have ready a large sheet titled: "Signs of the last age," and pictures to represent the signs and events, which are attached to the sheet as they are mentioned. You can use the pictures below.

Point out that we are in the last age at the moment, as we live between the Resurrection and the Second Coming.

Jesus warned his friends that this would be a difficult and dangerous age to live in and stay faithful to God. And that is true. Since Jesus said these words, lots of his followers have been arrested and imprisoned.

At this point, have a leader bursting into the room with some plastic handcuffs, without smiling, and very officious. Is there a Thomas Godshill here? They have reason to believe that this man is a Christian and they've come to arrest him. The other leaders protest, in a frightened way, that there aren't any Christians here, but Thomas (forewarned and primed, of course) stands out and proclaims that yes, he is a Christian, and worships the living God! The police angrily grab and arrest him, putting him in prison, behind a row of chairs.

Hopefully this episode will take the children by surprise so that they get a sense of danger, but without being unduly scared.

Jesus promised that though being his followers may involve getting teased or even imprisoned and tortured, we will always have Jesus' companionship, and "by standing firm, you will gain life."

Praying

O Jesus, I have promised
to serve thee to the end;
be thou for ever near me,
my Master and my friend;
I shall not fear the battle
if thou art by my side,
nor wander from the pathway
if thou wilt be my guide.

Activities

Make a group banner or poster to express the darkness and dangers, with candle flames of light to represent people living out good Christian lives in the middle of it. These form a winding path through the turmoil to a burst of light at the top of the picture.

Cross out the crosses to read Luke 21:12

Crack the Code

Luke 21:18–19

TQP HJHF JI PMFOF PMBHRO

ASH NFSEEX MSNG XJQ. TX

OPSHYBHR IBNG XJQ VBEE

RSBH EBIF.

CODE

A	B	C	D	E	F	G	H	I	J	K	L	M	N	O	P	Q	R	S	T	U	V	W	X	Y	Z
S	T	A	Y	F	I	R	M	B	C	D	E	G	H	J	K	L	N	O	P	Q	U	V	W	X	Z

To pray this week

O Jesus, I have promised
to serve thee to the end;
be thou for ever near me,
my Master and my friend:
I shall not fear the battle
if thou art by my side, nor
wander from the pathway
if thou wilt be my guide.

Christit the King

Thought for the day

This Jesus, dying by crucifixion between criminals, is the anointed King of all creation in whom all things are reconciled.

Readings

2 Samuel 5:1–3
Colossians 1:12–20
Luke 23:35–43

Aim: To explore the kind of King Jesus is.

Starter

What/who am I? Someone thinks of a person or thing, and the others ask questions to discover who or what it is. Only yes and no answers are allowed.

Teaching

In that game we were finding out more and more about the person or object until we were sure we knew who or what it was. Write the name "Jesus" in large letters in the middle of a sheet of paper and write around it all the things we have discovered about Jesus in our lives so far. Already we know quite a bit about him, and we are getting to know him in person as well. Encourage them to keep praying every day, and see if any of them still have a prayer habit, and are using their prayer corner that they made this year. If they've gotten a bit slack, help to get them going again.

Today we are celebrating Jesus Christ as King. What kind of a King is Jesus?

On another sheet, with a crown with Jesus' name on it in the middle, collect their ideas about this, prompting them if necessary with suggestions of things Jesus isn't, like bossy, proud, or greedy. Then draw a cross going through the crown; the cross is a better sign for our King because all the things we've written are to do with love, which he showed by dying for us on the cross.

Read them today's gospel to remind ourselves of just how loving and forgiving our King is.

Praying

When I survey the wondrous cross
on which the Prince of Glory died,
my richest gain I count but loss,
and pour contempt on all my pride.

Were the whole realm of nature mine
that were an offering far too small;
love so amazing, so divine,
demands my soul, my life, my all.

Activities

On the activity sheet there are instructions for making a jigsaw in which the central piece which holds the rest together is in the shape of a cross.

Notes

1 Cut out the rectangle. On the blank side, draw and color a picture of something which makes you very happy. Fill the whole page.

2 Cut up your picture along the lines shown; you should have 8 pieces.

3 Stick these pieces on thin card to make them strong.

4 As you put your puzzle together, remember that Jesus our king brings us back together with God. When we fall apart he puts us together again.

Dictionary

Survey – look at

Contempt – scorn, something you don't think much of

Realm – kingdom   Offering – a present

Divine – just like God   Demands – asks

To pray this week

When I survey the wondrous cross
on which the Prince of Glory died,
my richest gain I count but loss,
and pour contempt on all my pride.
Were the whole realm of nature mine
that were an offering far too small;
love so amazing, so divine,
demands my soul, my life, my all.

Jesus draws us together with God again.